PRAISE FOR *Can't Make This Stuff Up!*

"Susannah Lewis's book is a girlfriend's call to live better, freer, and like someone loved you enough to die for you. Susannah doesn't yell at you, or shame you . . . she nudges you through humor and sarcasm and storytelling, which is pretty much the only way a person can get through to me anyway. So I love her!"
—Melissa Radke, author of *Eat Cake. Be Brave.*

"*Can't Make This Stuff Up!* is like a warm homemade biscuit with some apple butter on top for the soul. Susanna delivers practical Southern wisdom with her signature hilarious twist in every chapter. Her transparency and honesty are unfiltered, which is refreshing in a world where so much is!"
—Autumn Miles, author of *I Am Rahab*

"Have mercy, y'all. This book. I absolutely adore it, and you will too. You will laugh, you will nod your head, you will laugh, you will talk back, and you will laugh some more. But let me assure you of this: underneath the funny stories and the entertaining cast-of-characters (and oh, are there ever some characters), there is so much substance in these pages. This is a book you'll read and reread and read out loud—one that you'll go back to when you need encouragement, when you need to smile, and when you need to remember that God is in every detail of this beautiful life. Susannah is honest, she's hilarious, and she wouldn't recognize pretense if it walked up to her in the middle of the grocery store and tried to hug her neck. More than anything, though, she has a knack for finding Jesus way deep down in the ordinary, and by the end of this book, you'll not only know Susannah better—you'll want to know Him more."
—Sophie Hudson, author of *Giddy Up, Eunice*, and cohost of *The Big Boo Cast*

"Reads like a trip down memory lane with an old friend. You know those songs, movies, or even smells that bring back a warm and joyful memory from your past? That's what Susannah's stories are like. If I wasn't giggling through the chapters, I was smiling ear to ear as her memories and experiences had me right back in my own Southern childhood home. Such a well-written, enjoyable, relatable read start to finish!"

—Carolanne Miljavac, author of *Odd(ly) Enough*

Can't Make This Stuff Up!

Finding the Upside to Life's Downs

SUSANNAH B. LEWIS

NELSON
BOOKS

An Imprint of Thomas Nelson

Published in Nashville, Tennessee, by Nelson Books, an imprint of Thomas Nelson. Nelson Books and Thomas Nelson are registered trademarks of HarperCollins Christian Publishing, Inc.

Published in association with Jessica Kirkland and the literary agency of Kirkland Media Management, LLC, P.O. Box 1539, Liberty, TX 77575.

Thomas Nelson titles may be purchased in bulk for educational, business, fund-raising, or sales promotional use. For information, please e-mail SpecialMarkets@ThomasNelson.com.

Unless otherwise noted, Scripture quotations are taken from the Holy Bible, New International Version®, NIV®. Copyright © 1973, 1978, 1984, 2011 by Biblica, Inc.® Used by permission of Zondervan. All rights reserved worldwide. www.Zondervan.com. The "NIV" and "New International Version" are trademarks registered in the United States Patent and Trademark Office by Biblica, Inc.®

Scripture quotations marked ESV are from the ESV® Bible (The Holy Bible, English Standard Version®). Copyright © 2001 by Crossway, a publishing ministry of Good News Publishers. Used by permission. All rights reserved.

Scripture quotations marked NASB are from New American Standard Bible®. Copyright © 1960, 1962, 1963, 1968, 1971, 1972, 1973, 1975, 1977, 1995 by The Lockman Foundation. Used by permission. (www.Lockman.org)

Scripture quotations marked AMPC are from the Amplified Bible, Classic Edition. Copyright © 1954, 1958, 1962, 1964, 1965, 1987 by The Lockman Foundation. Used by permission. (www.Lockman.org)

Scripture quotations marked NKJV are from the New King James Version®. © 1982 by Thomas Nelson. Used by permission. All rights reserved.

Any Internet addresses, phone numbers, or company or product information printed in this book are offered as a resource and are not intended in any way to be or to imply an endorsement by Thomas Nelson, nor does Thomas Nelson vouch for the existence, content, or services of these sites, phone numbers, companies, or products beyond the life of this book.

ISBN 978-1-4002-0802-9 (eBook)

Library of Congress Cataloging-in-Publication Data

Names: Lewis, Susannah B., 1981- author.
Title: Can't make this stuff up! : finding the upside to life's downs / Susannah B. Lewis.
Description: Nashville : Thomas Nelson, 2019. |
Identifiers: LCCN 2018036135 (print) | LCCN 2018054106 (ebook) | ISBN 9781400208029 (e-book) | ISBN 9781400208012 (pbk.)
Subjects: LCSH: Lewis, Susannah B., 1981- | Christian biography--United States. | Christian life--Anecdotes.
Classification: LCC BR1725.L4355 (ebook) | LCC BR1725.L4355 A3 2019 (print) | DDC 277.3/083092 [B] --dc23
LC record available at https://lccn.loc.gov/2018036135

Printed in the United States of America

19 20 21 22 23 LSC 10 9 8 7 6 5 4 3 2 1

To my parents in heaven who are making angels laugh.
To my children, NA and BB, who make me laugh.
To the mean girls in middle school who
pointed at me and laughed.
Thank you.

Contents

CONTENTS

Foreword

The South—the place where mud pies are a neighborhood delicacy and sweet tea keeps dentists in business for the duration. It is the place where I learned how to drive a 4x4, use a crockpot, and most importantly, where I learned the word *ain't*. Growing up in "the country" is simple living at its best, and if you haven't been, quite frankly, you haven't lived.

Susannah and I grew up just a few miles apart, but it wasn't until adulthood that we became partners in crime. Even though our growing-up years had us in separate circles I can promise you this, the stories in this book are as accurate as a Sunday morning tithe-and-offering count. You know why? Because she's right—you can't make this stuff up! When I read these pages I was immediately taken back to my Southern childhood and I found my own little-girl self inside the stories of this book. She transported me back in time and reminded me of the goodness that is Southern living.

Susannah Lewis . . . she just has a way. Her ability to story-tell draws you in and sits you down at the table of her life—right there beside her mama's casserole dishes and stained Tupperware bowls. Her endearing honesty, sassy wit, and tender heart give you a glimpse into her Tennessee upbringing—the beauty and the heartache—and leave you with all the Southern feels. The life stories she tells and life lessons she's learned will bring a smile to your face and tears to your eyes. By the end of this read, if you haven't made a pecan pie or bought a mono-grammed decal for the back window of your vehicle, I question your salvation.

Happy reading, everyone.

And welcome home.

Welcome to the South.

Heather Land
"I Ain't Doin It"

Hey, Y'all!

Welcome to the South.

(Yes, I capitalize South, and by golly I always will.)

I'm often appalled at the way my region is depicted in movies and on television. The other night I came across a reality show where the guests at an Alabama wedding reception started mud wrestling. As someone who has lived down South all my life, let me assure you I've never witnessed such a debacle. I have seen a groom stand on a picnic table in his bare feet and belt out Garth Brooks's "Shameless" into a beer bottle, but there was certainly no mud involved, okay?

And I've never (*read: only once*) had a cousin arrested

for unlawfully trespassing on a mountainside to dig up ginseng. All (*read: most*) of my relatives have all their teeth and none (*read: only a few*) have allowed a Marlboro to dangle from their lips while they put five dollars of gas in their Chevrolet Beretta sporting four spare tires. But, contrary to popular belief, it isn't customary for Southerners to wed our uncles' sons or wear thongs to the Fourth of July picnic.

Okay, I'll admit that I have seen an above ground pool inside a garage, therefore making it an indoor above ground pool. I've seen grown men cry at NASCAR defeats. I've seen a recliner strapped to the top of a Geo Metro. I know someone named Tickle. I know someone named Skeeter. And yes, Skeeter's stepson, Catfish, once pulled my 4x4 truck out of a ditch.

Heavens, I've seen some things.

But, the truth is, down South, you'll find good-hearted, hardworking people who respect their elders. There's sweet tea in every refrigerator and piping hot pies on Grandma's windowsill. Old men rock on wraparound porches they share with lazy dogs, and neighbors bring over casseroles when your mama is sick. There's a heavy-set preacher shouting the gospel from behind a pulpit and wiping his sweaty brow with a handkerchief.

You'll find kids with Kool-Aid mustaches chasing each other around shady magnolia trees (and tripping over the massive roots). Lakes are crowded with fishing boats, mosquitoes are the size of canaries, and crickets are the size of frogs. Old ladies gossip beneath hair dryers at the Cut N' Curl. There is a fruit and vegetable stand on the corner of every highway. You'll see after-church spreads of fried chicken, mashed potatoes, and okra on dining tables covered in generations-old tablecloths.

You'll find hydrangea and honeysuckle bushes spilling onto sidewalks. There's a storyteller or two at every family reunion. Grandma's tattered cookbook rests next to the family Bible and a worn apron hangs on the hook by the kitchen screen door. You'll find kindness and manners and respect, and the works of Tennessee Williams, William Faulkner, and Flannery O'Connor on bookshelves. Things move a little slower down South, but that's just fine by us.

In the South, you'll also find me—an orphaned thirty-seven-year-old wife and mother, born and raised in a small Tennessee town, clinging to the promises of God and looking for every opportunity to laugh. I spray Shout on unidentifiable stains daily and wear monogrammed pullovers while hauling kids to ball practice in an SUV that smells like a locker room. I sit in my back-porch swing, in awe of God's stunning sunsets, with a laptop by my side. I'm often on social media sharing unbelievable shenanigans that take place in my home, childhood memories that will forever bring a smile to my face, and the beautiful promises that the Lord has so graciously spoken to my heart.

This is my world. This is my South.

If you think the South sounds pretty good, stick around as I pass on some of the Southern wit and wisdom I am so thankful was passed along to me. You'll see purpose revealed through pain and beauty springing forth from ashes. If that doesn't sound good to you, well, I'll just put on my Ray-Bans, douse my hair in anti-humidity hairspray, and bless your little ole heart.

CHAPTER 1

Write, Rinse, Repeat

My mother was quite the storyteller. Whether humorous fiction or factual accounts of her youth, her stories captivated me, molded me, and planted a seed within me that would one day grow into a calling.

Mama began filling my head with tales when I was just a little girl. She sat on the edge of my canopy bed, stroked my long hair, and wove a humorous plot about Farmer Brown's wife and the chickens that flew through her kitchen window. What a mess they made in poor Mrs. Brown's farmhouse. Those foul fowl wreaked havoc. Silly chickens were the last thought I had before drifting off to sleep.

I also heard numerous anecdotes while I rode in the passenger seat of my mother's Oldsmobile. She'd point to places in our hometown and tell stories about them. I still know the exact spot where she fell off her bicycle on College Street and will never forget the harrowing tale of the drifter who jumped off the train on Boyd Avenue, banged on her aunt Ottie's back door, and paced the porch whistling an eerie tune. I'll forever picture the older couple who lived on Washington Avenue and were terrified their new color television was going to damage their eyes, so they wore sunglasses. I would laugh so hard that I snorted when Mama regaled us with the tale of visiting them and being forced to put on dark glasses to watch *Gunsmoke*.

I especially loved to hear my mother talk about the summers she spent with her refined and elegant Aunt Nancy on Fairfax Avenue in Nashville. Aunt Nancy was a beautiful woman who wore diamonds and sapphires and loathed dirt. She went so far as to wrap newspaper around the gas and brake pedals in her car to keep them spotless. Aunt Nancy was also often embarrassed by her husband James's lack of filter. Mama loved to recount the time Uncle James told a chatty dinner guest to "quit talking and start chewing" while Aunt Nancy turned twenty-four shades of crimson and my young mother covered her face with her napkin to stifle her laughter.

And Lord have mercy, I'll never forget the story about Betsy.

Betsy went to school with my mother and lived in a beautiful house on the hill near the high school. On her way home from school, Mama passed right by Betsy's house where Betsy's mother kept her 1959 Impala parked on the street out front. Betsy was not quite old enough to drive, but she would sit inside that car, and each time someone passed her house she'd pump the brakes so it seemed that she'd just parked the massive Chevrolet. She spent many afternoons doing this just so her classmates would think her parents allowed her to drive. Mama said sometimes Betsy would honk the horn and wave too. That visual of young Betsy trying her best to fit in with the older kids will forever live in my mind.

I'd always loved hearing my mother's stories, but it never occurred to me to write my own until I was eight years old. I had checked out a book at my elementary school library called *The Trouble with Tuck*. I vividly remember the picture on the cover: a dog and a girl sitting under a tree. The girl's shirt was tucked into terribly short shorts, and it looked awful uncomfortable, so I thought maybe the trouble she was having was with that shirt *tucked* into those tiny shorts, but after reading the back cover, I realized that Tuck was the dog. And as a dog lover, I was sold. I took the book home, not knowing it would change my life.

I was lying on my bedroom floor, a chubby kid with a Little Debbie in one hand and the book in the other, when I reached the part where Tuck went blind. Tears poured from my eyes and dampened the pages. I was terrified I was going to get in trouble for soaking (and getting Fudge Round on) those pages by our strict librarian who kept a wooden paddle with holes drilled in it on her desk. But once the fear subsided, I realized something beautiful had happened. That book made me feel something. It brought me joy and laughter as I read about the little girl and her best friend going on adventures, and then the book made me cry my eyes out. Right then I decided that's what I wanted to do. I wanted to write books. Not books about blind dogs per se, but books that made people feel something.

So I started a little series of stories about two friends named Laura and Sarah. On notebook paper, I penned the tale of their friendship and elementary school escapades. I illustrated the covers with stick people, my only illustrative talent, and stapled the pages together. Then I wrote rave reviews on the back and drew *New York Times* bestseller stamps on them. Hey, go big or go home, right?

I loved writing so much I decided to give novels a try. I penned *twenty whole pages* about a girl and her mother who were chased by a truck driver. I cranked out a tale about a haunted garage and another about a kid with the superpower to make things smell like strawberries. I got so lost in those stories every day after school that I forgot to do my homework, but I had found my calling. Math homework did not matter. (Until I got my report card.)

When I was eleven and my father died, I discovered writing was cathartic and therapeutic. I could feel my burdens being lifted when I wrote about the pain and the void that accompanied my daddy's sudden passing. As I banged out words on my Brother typewriter, I recognized writing was so much more than a hobby.

I stuck with it. I was late for high school many mornings because I'd stayed up late writing a book about some zit-faced boy who'd thrown me over for a girl with prettier bangs. I lost interest in other hobbies (I knew basketball wasn't for me when I kept trying to make shots in the wrong goal), but I remained passionate about the written word. And, after graduation, I went to college and took creative writing courses to hone my craft. I was delighted when my writing professors left words of affirmation on my essays. (My math professors did the opposite—in red ink.) I was confident writing really was what I was meant to do.

A few years ago, I wrote a short story that took place in the South in the 1950s. It was about forbidden love between a poor girl and the rich boy across town. Sweet Caroline, in her hand-me-down dresses, wanted only to be accepted by John Williams's prominent family. I read that story to my mama, and when I looked over at her, her cheeks were damp with tears.

"Mama, what is it? Are you all right?"

"You're a fabulous storyteller, Susannah," she said. "You have a gift. What you've written there—that's art."

What my mother had done—what my grandmothers and great aunts had done when they were sitting in rocking chairs recounting memories and embellishing them along the way—was art. It was a gift.

James 1:17 says, "Every good and perfect gift is from above." I thanked God for it.

While staying at home with two children under the age of four, I started a blog called *Write, Rinse, Repeat*. I thought that was a really clever name because I wrote, and I rinsed recycled Similac from bibs and couches and the dog, and I did it all over again. Every. Single. Day.

As my children napped, I logged on to my blog and wrote about daily life as a stay-at-home mother. I wrote about the mundane. I penned humorous tales about trips to the grocery store, the piles of laundry, and the song "Elmo's Potty Time" relentlessly running through my mind when I rested my head on my pillow at the end of a long day. I'm pretty sure Mama and my sister, Carmen, were the only two souls who read my blog posts, but I wasn't writing to gain popularity. I was writing because it was freeing to craft words about the fun of parenting and even the frustration of not having adult conversation.

I self-published several novels and short stories. I won some writing contests and was assigned a column for the local newspaper. And I loved every moment of it. I loved being stopped in Target to talk about the characters in my books as if they were real people. I still wasn't writing for popularity, but it was incredibly surreal that I finally had a platform and my words had an impact on strangers. I was grateful I'd made people feel something, just as I'd set out to do after I read *The Trouble with Tuck* so many years ago.

As I went through my mother's belongings in the weeks after she passed away, I found a copy of a novel she'd been working on for nearly a decade. She never finished it, but I read the words in her beautiful penmanship and thought, *This will live on forever.* That's the beautiful thing about stories. Long after we're gone, the stories last. They are passed down from generation to generation. They are spoken around campfires and on front porches and as a mother strokes her daughter's hair. They are imperishable.

Then my precious mama died. I was so consumed by grief I couldn't bear to write anything humorous. And that's what I was known for—I had been called the "modern-day Erma Bombeck." People visited my blog for a daily laugh. I did not want to disappoint my followers, but I had to write what I was feeling.

So I wrote about my mama's death. The words were real and raw, and I had no idea how many people they would resonate with, but I didn't care. I had to release the pain, so I wrote nearly every day. I wrote as the movers hauled my mother's baby grand piano out of her living room, and as I soaked in the silence of what was once a loud, lively home. I wrote about the denial, the regret, the longing, the void. My fingers rapidly pounded on my keyboard, and tears streamed from my eyes. I left my torn heart on that computer screen.

As the comments and emails poured in, I learned grief is a universal language. Because we live in a fallen world, everyone has experienced pain, longing, and despair. God comforted my broken heart, and then it was as if He put His hand on mine and we wrote words of encouragement and hope together. I understood what Peter said in 1 Peter 4:10, "Each of you should use whatever gift you have received to serve others, as faithful stewards of God's grace in its various forms."

And this was God's perfect plan from the beginning. Isaiah 25:1 says, "Lord, you are my God; I will exalt you and praise your name, for in perfect faithfulness you have done wonderful things, things planned long ago."

Things planned long ago.

When my mother told me the stories about fairies and farmers and sweet Betsy, as I read a book about a blind dog, as my platform grew, God knew all along one day my words would have purpose and comfort others. He had it all planned out.

I look back on the events in my life—the happiness and sadness and loss and redemption and restoration—and it's like a book. God is writing the story of my life. He's writing the story of *your* life. And just like any great read, there has to be plot development. There has to be a test for the testimony. Things have to happen or it would be a snooze fest, wouldn't it? Sometimes the story leaves us crying. Or on the edge of our seats. Or laughing. Or pee-ing our pants. Or wondering what is going to happen next. But the characters always have purpose.

When I write fiction, I am in control of the story. I never fear for my characters. I never think, *Well, I'm going to allow her to go through some things, and I sure hope she perseveres!* No, I already know how the story ends. I'm bigger than the protagonist's problems. I can squash the antagonist with one word. I'm the author. I'm in control.

Just as God is the Author of our stories—of our lives.

Embrace that. Embrace your purpose and trust the Author.

And you know what else I've discovered? God not only writes our story, He rinses us of our sins. He writes. He rinses us white. He writes. He rinses. And repeats.

CHAPTER 2

Cry So Hard You Laugh

It was Christmas morning, 1989.

My mother sat on the arm of our corduroy couch in her bathrobe stained with dollops of Clairol natural blonde hair color. She yawned and sipped from her coffee mug while I raved over my new *Who Framed Roger Rabbit* VHS tape. My brother and sister, ages twenty-three and twenty, no longer enamored with opening gifts at the butt-crack of dawn, still slept in their beds.

My dad searched beneath the tree for Mama's gift. He finally handed her a present he'd purchased the night before, concealed not by paper sporting trees or snowflakes or Santa, but rather the sack from the store. My daddy always did things at the last minute, but he managed to get them done.

"Merry Christmas!" He handed her the plastic bag with a knot tied at the top.

My mother sarcastically remarked at the lovely wrapping paper while she put her mug on the coffee table and tucked her bouncy, blonde Farrah Fawcett hair behind her ear. The plastic made a loud crinkling sound as she pulled out a ladies' electric razor and examined it closely.

"It's an Epilady!" my dad exclaimed. "That's what you wanted, isn't it?"

"Yes, Billy Brown, but it's not even in a box." The device's long cord dropped to the floor.

"I know, Susan Ann, but it was the only one they had. It's the display model," he answered.

"Oh . . . thanks!" She continued to eye the pastel purple razor. "But it's got hair in it."

The steam from Mama's hot cup of coffee mixed with the smoke of my dad's Vantage cigarette in the ashtray as she held the used razor. Daddy turned as red as the tinsel on our tree when he realized what a terrible (and disgusting) Christmas present it had turned out to be.

I know all those vivid details because that moment was being recorded. When I dig out the antique VCR and watch the VHS tape of Christmas 1989, I see my pudgy eight-year-old body sitting on the living room floor in a New Kids on the Block T-shirt, soaking in the banter between my parents. I chuckle when my mother rants that every woman who walked through our local Service Merchandise in 1989 had touched that electric machete to her leg.

My mother and father had a tumultuous marriage at times, but they stuck it out for thirteen years. I truly believe if my father hadn't passed away suddenly when I was eleven years old, they would have continued to do so. Despite their frequent arguments over my father spending way too many hours at the country club bar, there was love between them. They drove each other crazy, but they were crazy in love.

Daddy was the disciplinarian, the one who told me to keep my eye on the ball, the one who spoiled me relentlessly, the one who provided the income to keep me in new Sam and Libby flats and Hypercolor T-shirts. He was the one who said he'd be in the trunk with a shotgun on my first date, the one who made me feel safe.

And when Daddy died, Mama mourned the love of her life, and yet she made his passing all about me—the fatherless child.

Mama tried to discipline me without caving to my pleas and promises. She poorly attempted to throw a curveball while I laughed. She went from being a stay-at-home mother to working crappy jobs for little pay. My mother paced the house alone and prayed for my safety during my rebellious years. My mother questioned the goofy perverted boys who showed up on the front door step. My mother made me feel safe in a world where daddies suddenly die and leave their children all alone.

Then my mother, my beautiful, precious, hilarious mother, went to bed on the night of September 19, 2015, with her suitcase packed at the foot of her bed for her upcoming trip to visit my sister and her family at their beach house in Destin, Florida. On her nightstand, there was a glass of water, a fingernail file, and my first book that she was so incredibly proud of and raved about on Facebook nearly every day. Her white noise machine softly played the "summer night" of crickets and bullfrogs. And sometime while she slept, her soul went to be with Jesus.

When she wouldn't answer the door to go with her boyfriend to church the next Sunday morning, he called me and said he was worried. I was home with my sick daughter, so I called my husband, Jason, who was at church. He drove across town to check on her. I became fearful and anxious, so I grabbed my Bible and opened it to the middle where I landed on the Twenty-Third Psalm. I sat on my bed and soaked in the promise that God was my comforter.

When Jason walked through our door about an hour later, I could see on his face that something was horribly wrong. All he could do was shake his head, his eyes clouded with tears, and say, "I'm sorry, Susannah."

It couldn't be. My mother wasn't ill. She wasn't old and feeble. She was supposed to drive eight hours down to the beach the next day. Old, feeble ladies don't go on long road trips to lie out on the sand and dance to Jimmy Buffett in a beachside restaurant. Jason's face confirmed my worst nightmare.

I fell to my knees. I didn't cry; that's not strong enough of a word. I wailed. My mother was dead, and I wailed.

When you lose one parent, it's like a comma. It slows things down. But when both of your parents are gone, it's a period. Final. Finished. And because I'd witnessed my daddy's death when I was eleven, I had an overwhelming fear of the period. I had often prayed God would allow me to die before my mother. That's how deeply I wanted to avoid the pain associated with the period—with being an orphan. Because no matter the age, when both of your parents are gone, you are an orphan. Just as helpless and lost in this world as a baby left on a doorstep, without an anchor. Without any roots.

To say I struggled with my mother's death would be an understatement. I was in such a deep pit of despair I could not see myself ever climbing out. I knew the Lord was close to my broken heart, but I was so clouded by grief that I couldn't adequately embrace that truth. I wanted to pick up the phone and call my mother, and I stared at her name in my phone with the overwhelming desire to press send. I wanted to hear her voice. I wanted to hear her laugh. I wanted to hear her play the piano. Mama used to pull me close to her and run her fingers through my hair and tell me, "Don't worry about a thing, sweet girl." That's what I needed. I craved my mother's presence so strongly that I couldn't bear to think of all the years I had left to live without her.

I think I was at the darkest point of my entire life when my sister, Carmen, and I faced the task of going through our mother's things. Rummaging through an entire house and picking through each drawer, cabinet, and closet was not only physically draining, but emotionally draining.

After a long week of packing and crying, I sat with my journal and wrote the following words:

How do you let go?

To each scrap of paper or photo or piece of clothing is attached a cherished memory. You come across placemats you've been looking at your entire life and have to make the painstaking decision to toss them in a donate box or keep them for another thirty years.

You keep them, of course.

And then you realize you're keeping too much stuff and have no place to put it all. The apron Mama wore is a must keep—no-brainer there—along with the furniture and knickknacks and twelve Rubbermaid bins of photos and family history and her poetry and three sets of fine China and the vintage light fixture that's been hanging over the kitchen table for decades. But what about that Tupperware from 1987 that carried her Mississippi mud cake to grandmother's house on birthdays and holidays? It still smells like her cake batter, but do you really need another piece of her Tupperware? Your kitchen cabinets are already over-flowing with her dishes.

So you toss the yellow cake carrier into the donate box and stew over it for the next hour. Should you have kept it? Should you keep every single one of her nightgowns, too, although you've already put four-teen of them in a box to take home? Can you let go?

You feel like she's there saying, "Don't get rid of that! That was your grandmother's mixing bowl! Are you really going to give away my favorite house shoes? I bought those at Goldsmith's ten years ago but they still look new!"

So you find yourself digging through the donate box for Tupperware and nightgowns and reading glasses and mixing bowls and house shoes and mag-nets from her refrigerator and you throw it all in your car.

You sit in your kitchen surrounded by boxes of your mother's makeup and spatulas and pillows and anything that still carries her scent. Suddenly you've inherited your deceased father's shirts and your deceased grandmother's kitchen towels because your mother couldn't let go of those things either.

You have no idea what to do with it all because these things don't fall into the "must keep" category the way her antique armoire and photos and the dress she wore to your wedding do. These things fall into the "can't yet let go" category.

You can't think about it anymore, so you shove it into closets and the attic. You'll do something with it all later.

Thirty years will pass and you'll still have boxes packed with Estée Lauder powder, SpellBound perfume, crusty blush brushes, placemats, and forty-year-old house shoes.

Cause you'll never want to let it go.

I wrote many similar journal entries over the course of several months. My words dripped with sorrow and longing and despair. The pages of that journal are wrinkled from my tears. I often sat over that leather book and cried so hard that snot poured out of my face like the chick on *The Blair Witch Project*.

And one night, while sitting on my closet floor and overcome with sadness and craving my mother's presence more than I could bear, I thought about that Epilady razor. I thought of that disgusting used Epilady with some stranger's hair dangling from the blade, and I laughed. It was the strangest thing, because I was sobbing uncontrollably at the same time. I didn't even know it was possible to do both. (And let me tell you, laughing and crying simultaneously makes a real weird noise.)

Life is like that sometimes, though, isn't it? We can be consumed by many different emotions, and exhausted by them all. We can be overwhelmed with sharp, jagged grief—an immeasurable void—but a pleasant memory is capable of bringing us a little joy even if only for a moment. I like to think the Lord placed that very memory on my mind at that very moment to cheer me up. Maybe, just maybe, God led my father to that used, hairy razor with me, twenty-six years later, in mind.

We have to choose joy. The Holy Spirit has already infused us with it, but we have to reach down and grab it and utilize it. Sometimes joy is stubborn and just won't surface, but it's there. And we have to say, "Hey, Joy! Get your butt over here! I need you right now! And bring your buddy Laughter with you!" And then we have to cling to it for dear life. We have to take that spark of happiness and fan the flame.

It's no mistake I grew up in a witty household. I think every hairy razor and possessed stray cat was placed in my path for a reason. Those recollections, along with the precious and unfailing comfort of Christ, are what continue to see me through the hard times.

Proverbs 17:22 says, "A cheerful heart is good medicine, but a crushed spirit dries up the bones." So, basically, if we don't cheer up, we're going to dry up. And I don't know about you, but I'm not interested in drying up. That's why I use moisturizer every night. And why I choose cheerfulness.

We are called to think on what is noble, pure, and lovely (Philippians 4:8). On the good things. On brighter days. To push through the sadness and search for joy.

Find it. Grab it. Hold on to it for dear life.

And you might just cry so hard you laugh.

CHAPTER 3

Love the Ones You're With

When I was in high school, my principal called me to the office just to tell me the decades-old story of my sixteen-year-old daddy riding on a train from our small town of Brownsville, Tennessee, to Memphis. Daddy had the bright idea to hop on the train and ride it from one side of our small town to the other, but it picked up full speed and went on a fifty-mile journey. Like a locomotive-riding cowboy, he used his belt to strap onto a ladder on the side of the train for the long, freezing trek. When he finally arrived in Memphis, he was so cold he went into a Laundromat by the railroad tracks to get warm. He kept putting money into the dryer to heat his hands, but every time he opened the dryer door, it turned off.

My principal loved telling me that story, but my grandfather, who had to drive down to Memphis in the middle of the night to pick up my teenaged daddy, didn't as much.

He never rode on the outside of another train, but Daddy was always doing or saying something silly. He was known for his quick wit, one-liners, and ability to make everyone laugh. As a child, I remember looking up his tall, thin frame to watch him talking as all the men surrounding him laughed heartily. He knew a hundred old jokes and made up a hundred of his own. His sense of humor was brilliant, and I'm still reminded of it anytime I run into one of his old friends, who recounts a memory of my father. He was also known for carrying a huge video camera around and making hilarious skits that were SNL-worthy. He did YouTube before YouTube was even a thing.

Daddy wasn't just a tall, funny guy with a mustache that rivaled Tom Selleck's. He was also a collector. He worked for the telephone company and often brought home things he found in the crawl spaces of homes. We had a stockpile of old Coke bottles he'd come across, antique tools, and even a Buddy Holly 45 record, but he also brought home countless strays. Mama liked dogs, so she tolerated the many he decided to adopt. But she drew the line at cats. Cats scared her.

"I don't like any animal I can't hear coming," she said.

Stephen King's classic *Cat's Eye* sealed the deal for her, though. After watching the movie, she was convinced those furry felines sucked the breath out of people while they slept.

So one summer day on his lunch break, Daddy brought home what mother called the "black spawn of Satan." I will never forget, at age eight or nine, watching that ebony cat clawing the cushions on the wicker sofa in our sunroom. Daddy had dropped him off only ten minutes before, against my mother's wishes and pleas, and that cat scratched and strewed stuffing all over the floor like a four-legged psycho. Once he was done with the poor floral cushions, he shot straight up the pleated curtains that framed the French doors on the back of the house and perched there, hissing, like something straight out of a horror movie. My mother, the godly woman she was, cried out to Jesus for help. She literally cried out for Jesus to remove the "black spawn of Satan" from our dwelling. Finally, armed with a broom and a cordless phone (in case she needed to dial 911), she threw open the French door and let out a bloodcurdling scream when the feline from hell charged at her, teeth showing, before disappearing into the woods behind our home.

Daddy never knew the true story about how that cat disappeared. Mama just told him it "got away" when she opened the door to go outside. He quickly found a replacement, though. I think he brought home a new cat a few days later. It wasn't quite the "spawn of Satan," but it eventually managed to "get away" too.

We never had a dull moment in our home, and I found it exhilarating. For my family, even a routine trip to the salon could be dramatic. I'll never forget falling to the kitchen floor and laughing until I nearly urinated on myself when my always-blonde mother walked through the door black-headed like Morticia Addams. Apparently her new hairstylist was "an idiot who is clearly on drugs and doesn't know the first thing about lowlights." And I'll never forget a run-of-the-mill fishing trip with my dad ending with the front two tires of his truck in the river.

Even our holidays weren't exempt from strange happenings.

One Thanksgiving, while dining on Mama's famous cornbread dressing (that's stuffing, Northern friends), a farm egg in her fall table centerpiece began to move. We immediately jumped up from our dining chairs while that egg, resting in a nest of decorative straw and cattails, cracked. Mama cried out to Jesus, and suddenly there was a baby chicken in the center of the table—*a dead baby chicken*. I am not well versed in biology, so I'm not sure how a dead chicken hatched, but how many people can say they've had a dead bird on their Thanksgiving table? Well, a lot. But how many can say it was a recently hatched dead baby chicken instead of a turkey? Not many.

This happened a few Thanksgivings after my father died, and my godfather, Mr. Charles, scooped that dead baby bird from the dining table with paper towels while my mother threw the entire centerpiece she'd worked on so diligently into the garbage can, put on rubber gloves, and disinfected the entire house with bleach. The whole meal was ruined, because who in the world can just resume eating turkey and mashed potatoes after a dramatic death scene?

The craziness wasn't just confined to our home, either. Visiting my aunt Cora and uncle Harvell's house was an adventure too.

Aunt Cora was always knocking on death's door. Bless her bones. I don't think she was ever admitted to the hospital, and she ended up living longer than half my relatives, but she constantly claimed she was being plagued with a new ailment, ache, or pain. When someone asked, "How are you doing, Aunt Cora?" she never answered, "Fine." Her feeble, little voice always responded with something like, "Well, my bursitis has flared up again and I have this horrible ringing in my left ear and the palpitations are getting worse and my knee is numb and hey, look here at this toenail. Does it look ingrown to you?" Oh, but I adored Aunt Cora. I adored the way her rouge settled into the deep wrinkles on her cheeks. I adored her perfume-laden hugs. And I adored the homemade zucchini bread she served on daisy-covered plates. Yes, Aunt Cora complained a lot, but the one thing Aunt Cora never grumbled about was her beloved dog, a black-and-white feist named Lady.

The name was ironic because Lady was no lady. She was ten pounds of terror. She snarled and growled and usually had to be put in the laundry room when guests came over because, as Aunt Cora, explained, "She gets real excited when company comes, and no one knows what she'll do." Except we all knew what Lady would do. She tried to decapitate anyone who walked through the door, even Aunt Cora. Aunt Cora would call, "Come here, sweet Lady," in her feeble little voice, and Lady would charge her and grab hold of her panty hose and tug until they unraveled. Lady would gnaw on Aunt Cora's liver-spotted arms until blood trickled from them. And she'd just say, "Oh, sweet Lady. You're being too rough." It was downright horrifying, yet comical, to watch this dog constantly attacking an eighty-year-old woman, but Aunt Cora never complained about the dog. Not once. (Uncle Harvell would wink at me before he intentionally turned down his Beltone so he couldn't hear Aunt Cora's complaints or Lady growling and gnawing on his artificial leg.)

Because I grew up among crazy, humorous people and crazy, humorous events, I often felt as if I were living in a sitcom. I truly believe the good Lord was preparing my heart for things to come when He gave me those relatives and infused our household with humor. He knew during my darkest moments of depression and despair, I would recall a memory of my youth—the frog in the bathroom or the pressure cooker blowing up and nearly obliterating us all—and my burden would suddenly become lighter. He knew I would cling to those memories—I would need those memories—when eventually most of my relatives were buried on a shady, cool hill on the southwest side of town.

When I think about my childhood and the summer nights in my mother's plush bed, as the box fan roared and crickets chirped outside her open bedroom window, I am immediately blanketed in peace. *Knot's Landing* played quietly on the Quasar television while Mama, the godly woman she was, lit a Winston Ultra-Light 100 and the ceiling fan swirled smoke around her wallpapered bedroom. I'd rest my head by her feet as she shared stories with me about her baby sister. Aunt Linda had been killed by a drunk driver when she was twenty-one, but tears of laughter streamed down my mama's face as she recollected fun memories of their youth, their Collie dogs, and being dragged along on sales calls with my granddaddy, the Watkins salesman. I realize now Mama shared those stories with me because they kept her sister alive. Although Mama was heartbroken over her sister's death for so many years, her memories and the stories of her youth restored some joy to her heart. And even though I'd never met my aunt Linda, I felt as if I knew her.

That's the very reason I find myself telling you— telling anyone—tales about my childhood. Those crazy stories about the cat and the hatching egg and the train all keep my parents alive. Memories keep my beloved people alive. And that's a beautiful thing, isn't it?

Now that I'm a mother, I have adopted my own version of storytelling in one particular way that my children appreciate: silly songs. I hate to toot my own horn, but I'm pretty good at making up silly songs. I can take any pop song from the eighties and twist the lyrics for whatever situation I'm in. For example, when my husband passes gas, I can break into a chorus of "Don't You Fart on Me," which is a parody of Simple Minds' "Don't You Forget About Me." And I can go way beyond just the chorus. I can twist that entire song into two solid minutes about spousal flatulence. My seven-year-old son, Bennett, loves this about me. We often make up songs about our dogs, Nutella, Pepper, Tucker, and Bailey. (Yes, four dogs. I want one or two more, but I also want to stay married.) I find so much joy singing with the radio and looking in my rearview mirror to see my little boy laughing so hard no sound comes out. When he finally catches his breath, he says, "Mama, make up another song!"

One day, when I'm long dead and gone, Bennett is going to remember that. He's going to remember how I turned "Rosanna" by Toto into "Nutella." When he and his own children are flying around in their Jetsons car, "Rosanna" will come on the oldies station and he will sing, "All I want to do is run and wag my tail and play all day. Nuteeeeeella, yeah!" He'll be taken back to that joyful moment when he was seven and laughed so hard no sound came out.

God knows we need our people. He makes our

children solely for us, just as He made us for our parents. He knows the vision of our grandmother sitting on the edge of the bed in a mint-green hairnet while slathering Vicks on her neck molds us in some way. He knows the scent of our mother's hair and the feeling of our father's stubble on our cheek when he kisses us leaves a lasting imprint on us. He knows our uncle's wink and our aunt's love for a killer feist is something that will bring a little joy to our heart amid our darkest moments.

I long to rest at my mother's feet in that wallpapered bedroom while she tells me a story about Brownsville, Tennessee, in 1960. I long to ride shotgun in my daddy's Chevrolet Silverado while his golf clubs sling around in the bed and Bob Dylan plays on the radio. I want Granny to fry up some salmon patties while she dances to bluegrass gospel in her kitchen. I want to sit on that creaky front-porch swing and rest my head on my great-grandmother's shoulder while a Popsicle melts down my arms.

But I can't. That time in my life is over. I won't hear their voices or hold them in my arms until we meet in heaven, but I'm so thankful I embraced every moment. That so many wild, crazy adventures took place in our home. That I memorized so many old stories. That my mother's laugh and my grandmother's wrinkled hands are forever engrained in my memory and will help carry me through the rest of my time in this temporary home. We weren't the perfect family, as you'll see, but I'm so glad God gave me those amazing people, those humorous people, faults and hang-ups and all.

You may not have chosen your people, but praise God, He chose the perfect people for you. Even if your uncle steals hubcaps and your lady cousin refuses to wax her beard, love them anyway. Embrace the time you're given with them. Cherish the moments.

Love the ones you're with.

CHAPTER 4

Tie a Knot Worth Tying

Picture it. December 31, 2001.

There was a tall, lanky guy standing in the corner of the bar. Every time I looked up, he was goofily grinning at me, and I assumed he was mesmerized by the glitter body spray I had so generously applied for the New Year's Eve festivities. He appeared to be a pretty cute kid, but I wanted to get a closer look. I needed to make sure he was not a "full-on Monet." Remember the 1995 classic movie *Clueless*? A Monet is "like a painting, see? From far away, it's okay, but up close, it's a big old mess."

I took a few steps closer, one of my dearest friends on my arm, and I was relieved to discover he was not a "full-on Monet." In fact, he was handsome. He had all his teeth, there were no visible weapons hanging from his pockets, there were no tattoos on his forehead, and his cologne wasn't overbearing. And most importantly, the boy was taller than me (I'm five foot eleven). I was immediately smitten.

As we danced to Prince's "Purple Rain" at that New Year's Eve party, I came really close to falling in love. I don't know if it was because he didn't step on my toes once or because I actually had to look up to see his eyes, but that very night, I walked him over to my brother, Keith, and I introduced him as, Jason, "your future brother-in-law." I imagine that was incredibly awkward for both Keith and the poor twenty-year-old kid I'd only known for about an hour, but I was right because we were, indeed, married in a quaint, country wedding chapel four years later. (This proves what I've known all along: I have ESP. I have predicted *Wheel of Fortune* winners before Pat even introduced the contestants.)

Moments before I walked down the aisle, countless older relatives who still call blush "rouge" gave me advice and wanted to be sure I knew marriage is not easy. And I was all, "Whatever, Grandma. I don't need your advice. We are in love. Love is never hard work. Being his wife will be a piece of cake. And speaking of cake, watch how good I'm going to shove a slice in his face at the reception."

Happily married for nearly twelve hours, we boarded

a cruise ship for our honeymoon. All giddy and in love, we sailed around Hurricane Rita on our way to the Bahamas and somewhere in the middle of the Atlantic, the good Lord decided to give us a souvenir: a baby.

Apparently, Dramamine is not a reliable form of birth control.

When I looked down at the positive pregnancy test only five weeks into our marriage, I was in absolute shock. When I showed Jason those two pink lines when he came home from work on that crisp October afternoon, I thought he was going to pass out and I was going to have to break out the smelling salts. We were excited, of course, but we also wanted to get into the groove of marriage and enjoy spending time together before a child was brought into the mix. God had different plans, as He often does.

We drove to Knoxville the following day to watch the Tennessee Volunteers play, and the ride was often silent. I was in the passenger's seat wondering if I was really ready to be a mother, and I'm positive Jason was terrified and somewhat anxious about becoming both a husband and father within the same year. I mean, he could barely grow a mustache and I could barely microwave a meal without scorching it. Were we ready to raise a child?

That cruise around Hurricane Rita foretold the difficulties to come. Like a raging storm, things were intense at times. It seemed a storm was always brewing beneath the roof of our first small home. I'd decorated with hand-me-down furniture (including a green sectional couch with built-in cupholders that I named Nessie because it reminded me of the Lochness Monster) and knickknacks from Dollar General. Being that Jason was a man-child and I a hormonal she-beast who craved chili-cheese tots at midnight, we argued constantly about finances and Jason's overwhelming desire to party and sing karaoke until 3:00 a.m. while I sat at home with nausea and heartburn.

In the early years of matrimony, our happiness continued to wax and wane. We spoke harsh words and made mistakes. I kept having visions of hitting him in the head with my grandmother's cast-iron skillet. Because he continually placed his glass on the coffee table without a coaster, I often mentioned divorce. I mentally itemized everything I wanted in the settlement, but he could keep the table with the drink ring.

At times I loathed Jason. At times I wondered if we'd made a colossal mistake in putting bands of white gold on each other's fingers. I drove to my mother's house many nights with a suitcase in the backseat next to a squirming baby because we'd had an argument and I wanted out. Mama had been married to a man who couldn't seem to grow up and would rather spend time with friends, playing golf and drinking a six-pack, than being a "family man." She often told me to hang in there for our daughter, Natalie Ann's sake. She told me to keep loving Jason and praying for him, and that's what I did.

But he wasn't the only one to blame for our marital

problems. Jason left tire marks in the driveway because he was so eager to get away from his nagging and disrespectful wife. I constantly yelled and screamed and talked to him like a dog. I sure wasn't a supportive and loving woman, so who could blame the poor guy for opting to sing Merle Haggard songs down at the local bar with a bottle in his hand instead of staying home with that she-beast?

The Enemy attacked our marriage fully, and we both threatened to leave the other more times than I can count, but we never did. We toughed it out. I refused to let the Enemy win. I knew the Lord brought us together (yes, He brought us together in a bar where we danced to Prince) and confirmed we were meant to be married when He blessed us with a child so soon after saying "I do," and I clung to that for dear life.

Fast-forward two children and thirteen years later, and I am in awe of how far Jason and I have come. What was once a marriage that consisted of yelling and sometimes downright disgust with each other is now completely different. Sure, our marriage still takes work (everyone's does), but we aren't doing it alone. We finally invited Jesus to be at the center of our union and vowed to pray for each other fervently, and the changes that have taken place in both of us can only be attributed to the Holy Spirit. I've watched a man who once ushered a twelve-pack down his throat every weekend become an usher at church, and a nagging and verbally abusive wife become one who speaks loving words of affirmation. I've watched a man who had the mouth of a sailor speak truth into seven-year-old boys in Sunday school. I've watched this man become the spiritual leader of our household by being the first one ready for church every Sunday and praying over our meals and speaking Scripture over our family. And the Lord gave me new appreciation and respect for Jason. I would never talk to him the way I did a decade ago. I cringe at the way I used to go off the deep end over the smallest things.

One day recently, I was particularly angry at Jason over something extremely petty. (I'd like to say I don't remember what it was, but I do. It involved a pair of boxer shorts lying on the floor precisely 1.2 centimeters from the hamper.) After stewing over it for nearly an hour, I made a choice. I made the choice not to have a full-blown come-apart and yell until our children and small animals scurried for cover. Instead, I fixed Jason lunch and took it to him on our back patio. I did not want to fix a sandwich for my beloved, and I even contemplated spitting in his Miracle Whip, but I fixed it anyway. And, listen y'all, he was so appreciative of the gesture. A little apprehensive at first, yes, but appreciative.

That was sacrificial love on my part, all right? Because I sacrificed a whole lot of pride making that ham and cheese sandwich for him after he had the audacity to leave his boxer shorts lying so close to the hamper.

I remember thinking, as he chomped on potato chips, *I love this man. Am I really going to ruin the entire day by arguing with him over boxer shorts lying 1.2 centimeters from the hamper? Really? They were so close. I mean, why didn't he just pick them up—no, Susannah. You aren't going to argue with him about this today.*

Years ago, I would have doused the boxer shorts in gasoline, set them on fire, and tossed them onto his lap.

Though many things, like Jason's lack of knowledge when loading the dishwasher, still infuriate me, and sometimes I have that vision of the cast-iron skillet coming into contact with his cranium, I rebuke that thought in the name of Jesus and we work through our issues. Why? Because God brought us together and God alone keeps us together. We are dedicated to praying for each other and for our marriage.

And, praise Almighty, I've taken the divorce lawyer off the speed dial.

A few years ago, I stood at the living room window and through tear-soaked eyes, I watched Jason bury my sixteen-year-old dog in the backyard. I saw him pause from shoveling dirt on Peaches's grave to wipe his damp face. My husband, the tough man that he is, was broken at my heartbreak. I knew right then that although he's going to make mistakes and I'm going to make mistakes, I have a good man who loves me, and that's something worth hanging on to.

We've weathered many storms by now. Jason is the one who prayed over me when my miscarriage was confirmed and I couldn't get out of bed for days. He's the one who celebrates my achievements and calls me out on my mistakes. He's the one who laughs when I laugh and holds me when I cry.

This is *agape* love. This is love at its ultimate. This is a love that sacrifices pride and self-interest. This is the love God has for us, which led Him to sacrifice His Son for our sins. This is the love Jesus possessed in order to obey His Father and sacrifice Himself. This is a love of supreme greatness.

You see, the Bible says the Enemy seeks to kill, steal, and destroy (John 10:10). And marriage is no exception. The Devil loathes *agape* love. He loathes the support and encouragement found in holy matrimony. He will get into our heads and lie to us about our spouses and our circumstances. He will tell us our husbands are awful because they aren't as romantic as the actor in some cheesy Hallmark movie. He will deceive us into believing we deserve better or everything is our husband's fault. He will refuse to let us see our own wrongs and instead prompt us to lash out at our spouses. This is why it is so important to be in the Word, have knowledge of the Holy Spirit, pray the full armor of God over our marriages, and invite Jesus to be at the center of them. Because Satan will do whatever he can to destroy what God has brought together.

Many times, marriages end because people fail to understand love is an action and not a feeling. It took me a long time to grasp that nugget from the Lord, but I'm so glad I finally did. That giddy "butterflies in my stomach" feeling I had when we danced to Prince so many years ago (which could have been the cheap champagne) isn't present every day, but this doesn't mean I don't love my husband. When will people realize feelings are fickle and fleeting, and love isn't intended to be that way?

Love is deliberate.

Love is on purpose.

It is also patient. It is kind. It does not envy. It does not boast. It is not rude or self-seeking. It is not easily angered and does not keep record of wrongs. And nowhere in 1 Corinthians 13 does it state love is a warm, fuzzy feeling.

When Jesus said in John 14:15, "If you love me, keep my commands," He was saying that loving Him is a deliberate action—not an emotional feeling. To love Jesus as He commanded, a conscious choice must be made to show love as described in 1 Corinthians 13, because Lord knows being patient, kind, and hopeful doesn't come naturally. It is a choice. We are expected to show love to our spouses always, even when we don't feel like it.

I'm talking to you, ladies, who have good men but are just bored with them or frustrated because they don't have the slightest clue how to use the vacuum or they don't write you poems or send flowers on random Thursdays, and you start to wonder if there is someone better out there. Listen, spouses aren't like cars. You can't just trade them in when you're sick of looking at their dashboards.

When the Lord brings two people together as one,

it is beautiful and sacred and worth fighting for. Let us guard our hearts. Let us guard our marriages. Let us keep God at the core of our relationship and show love even when our husbands leave boxer shorts lying 1.2 centimeters from the hamper.

And if we seek first that precious, flawless *agape* love—love that truly sacrifices, forgives, and believes (the love of Christ, freely given to those who ask and receive)—only then will we truly be able to love our spouses and withstand whatever comes our way.

CHAPTER 5

Bloom Where You're Planted

Sometimes I dream about the cracks in the sidewalk. The ones in my childhood hometown like the cavernous pit on Key Corner that always grabbed the front wheel of my skate and sent me plummeting to the hot asphalt. I'd get up, blood dripping down my leg, and continue my journey to the Exxon for a grape Slush Puppie on a hot summer afternoon.

Brownsville, Tennessee, is a small Southern speck on a map with population: not enough. The place where I spent my childhood. The place where my parents and grandparents spent their childhoods.

My great-grandmother, Bess Brown, once told me the town was named after our family. We'd founded the whole tiny place, "in all its boring glory," she said. She was 101 years old at the time and couldn't distinguish a car from a Coke can, but I believed her in my childish naïveté. I pedaled my hot pink Huffy bicycle through the neighborhood thinking, *This town is mine.*

My maternal granddaddy, Hilliard, owned the corner drugstore years before I was born, before emphysema riddled his body. I've seen pictures of the store, though, and how it looked like a place right out of Mayberry. My mama kept a few of the big glass bottles that had once contained Coke and grape syrup, and as a little girl, I'd stare at them and think about the old days in black and white when having a soda at a counter was a real "hoot." I remember the sound of the big trucks roaring by Hilliard and my grandmother Lucy's one-story Victorian cottage built in 1873. Those trucks shook the tall window panes and drowned out the sound of *Hee-Haw* on her rabbit-eared television.

My paternal grandmother, Rebecca Brown, was a favorite teller at the big bank with the indoor waterfall. She always gave me a handful of suckers when we visited, and then she strutted me around to show me off to all her friends. She made a bigger deal about me than necessary. I hadn't scored a single point in the church basketball game the prior night, but she made me out to be the next Wilt Chamberlain in pigtails and jelly shoes.

I spent summers carving graffiti (boys' names surrounded by hearts) on the back of her and my granddaddy Billy's shed. It was the same shed where my dad held band practice back in the sixties. Their claim to fame was wearing high-water pants and winning a talent show. I heard they could play "Gloria" like Van Morrison himself.

I remember the ugly red carpet in our church. It covered the altar where people wept and repented as a fat Southern preacher shouted about hell and damnation and wiped sweat from his brow. That bleeding red carpet soaked in the sounds of my mother, the pianist, banging out "When We All Get to Heaven" on the cherry baby grand.

When my granddaddy Billy died, I remember standing in the drafty funeral home and noticing my daddy slipping down the hallway. My mother motioned for me to follow him. I'll never forget finding him in a dark back room crowded with folding chairs and a dusty organ, and he was sitting on the floor weeping like a baby. That was the first time I'd ever seen my father cry.

My hometown. Where I heard names like Miss Fannie, Emma Tanna (Tanner pronounced "Tanna"), Mr. Parker, and I knew immediately who they were and every name that rested on the branches of their family tree. We all knew one another. I never went to a gas station, a diner, or a Peach Festival without my grandparents talking with ladies wearing too much blush or men with walking sticks about how so-and-so's boy just wasn't right after the war.

It was the little place where I could roam from one

end of town to the other on some set of wheels and never worry about kidnappers or scary guys in conversion vans. The place where I raced down a hill on a grocery cart and spilled onto Main Street and almost got hit by a Mack truck. I ran back into the grocery store to find my mama, my short life still flashing before my eyes. That store. I've memorized each aisle in that store. I can still see the big bell shaped like a cow that sat at the meat counter. "How may we serve moo?"

That town was the place where I ate too many ice cream cones and thick-cut bologna sandwiches. The place where I learned piano from a woman with the oldest, but prettiest, hands I'd ever seen—covered in wrinkles and spots, but nails always freshly painted peach. Her house smelled like old-lady powder, and I read my sheet music by the antique lamp on her upright.

That town was the old familiar place where we had family reunions in little cabins littered with sawdust on Tabernacle Road. Where the grown-ups drank iced tea and situated box fans to help ease the sweltering summer heat. Where the kids played hide-and-seek in a graveyard and I was too fat to hide behind the skinny tombstones.

But after I graduated high school, my mother and I packed our things and left. She left the town that had produced fifty years of memories for her. Granted, we only moved thirty miles from that small Southern speck on the map, but my father was dead, I had graduated school, and we felt it was time to leave. It was time to start new chapters in both our lives. It was time to live in a town that had a Target.

I went to college and majored in English and met a boy and we danced to Prince. We got married and had babies. You know that already, but guess where we ended up? A hop and a skip from his hometown. Not mine, but his.

We go to the diner after church, and the children and I are halfway done with our meals before Jason's taken the first bite. He's off gabbing with an old man with a yellow beard who took him fishing once when he was five. Jason had a crush on his granddaughter in elementary school. And he'll often try to explain to me who so-and-so is. "You know, she got married in high school. Her daddy was a dentist. You know her! She grew up on the four-lane!"

No, dear, I don't know who that is. Her father didn't fill my cavities.

Sometimes I look at the older women sitting on the church pew in front of me and imagine their backstories. I didn't grow up seeing their sweet faces or hearing my grandmother pray for their ailments. Those ladies aren't a part of my history. And then I get to thinking about my hometown again and how I knew everyone and always said a prayer for Mrs. Dora's migraines, and I mourn that a little. I don't necessarily want to live in Brownsville, Tennessee, again, but I cannot forget my childhood or the place where I was raised. And I miss thinking, although it was never necessarily true, *This town is mine.*

Please don't misunderstand. I love the town where I currently live. I have made many new friends and been blessed by numerous people here in my husband's neck of the woods, but sometimes as they discuss something unfamiliar that happened around here years ago, I realize this isn't really my town. Oh, I love this town. I really do love this town. But it isn't mine.

However, this *is* my children's hometown. Like the sidewalk cracks I so fondly remember, my daughter will someday dream of the wooded trails at the back of our property. My boy will remember the ball field where he would rather dig his cleats in the dirt than tag a kid on second. They'll remember their teachers, their mud pies, their bugs in Mason jars, their youth here in this small Southern speck on a map.

Every childhood trip to the corner grocery store, every time we pass the lumberyard and see old man Davis sweeping sawdust, every time we peer at the massive oak trees when we are at the stop sign on Park Street, we file that away, don't we? Isn't it funny how we can be lying in the bed one night, thinking about the wet towels that are still in the washing machine, and suddenly a vision of our eleventh-grade English teacher resurfaces? Wasn't she just precious (most of the time)? And how did she get her tight curls so blue?

Those memories define us in some way. Especially if we spent our childhoods in one place, whether it was a small community or a large, bustling city, we become one with that location on the map. The people, the stories, the sidewalks, the little old lady at church with the migraines—those things are all pieces to our innermost puzzle.

But often we are forced to leave the place that houses so many of our puzzle's pieces. This is because God moves us. He sends us. He transplants us.

Being transplanted can be intimidating. Letting go of the past to embrace a new beginning can seem downright impossible.

"Who am I if I'm not living in the cypress house on Thomas Street? Who am I if Stella doesn't do my hair? Who am I if I will never hug Mrs. Melba again? Who am I if I don't buy my vehicles from Mr. Kelso? Who am I if I never take a walk down this road again?" Those questions can leave us feeling a little out of place.

That's exactly how I felt when I left my hometown.

But I've learned I'm never in the wrong place to serve God.

Second Corinthians 2:14 says, "Thanks be to God who . . . through us diffuses the fragrance of His knowledge in every place" (NKJV).

You see that?

Every place.

Not just on Main Street in Your Hometown, USA.

Every place.

And God doesn't just do new "geographic" things. He doesn't just physically move us. He loves restoring and restarting and refreshing and renewing our lives. He loves to do a new thing within us.

Isaiah 43:18–19 reads, "Remember not the former things, nor consider the things of old. Behold, I am doing a new thing; now it springs forth, do you not perceive it? I will make a way in the wilderness and rivers in the desert" (ESV).

The Israelites were slaves and had lost everything, not to mention they were wondering when in the world God's promise would come to be. But they were instructed to forget the former things and see the new things God was doing. Like the dead leaves turning green again in spring, a new thing was *springing* forth. A rebirth was coming.

Physically moving from my hometown hasn't been the only new beginning in my life. When my mother passed away, I certainly didn't think of it as a new beginning. No, it seemed like the end. It was the end of our late-night talks and our laughter by the pool. No more of her homemade Mississippi mud cake on my birthday or Alfred Hitchcock marathons on her couch. My mother was gone from this temporary world and so many beautiful and precious things were finished. I thought my joy had come to an end too.

But I now recognize that her passing was, indeed, a new beginning. For her, it was the beginning of her eternal life in paradise resting at Christ's feet. And for me, it was time for God to do a new thing in my life even though it seemed painful and weird and foreign. It was time for me to learn to depend solely on Him instead of my mother. It was time for me to embrace His comfort, find my joy, and press on. It was time for me to grow in Him. And once I experienced His goodness through my grief, it was time to be on fire to spread His message of hope and encouragement.

Philippians 3:13–14 says, "Brothers, I do not consider that I have made it my own. But one thing I do: forgetting what lies behind and straining forward to what lies ahead, I press on toward the goal for the prize of the upward call of God in Christ Jesus" (ESV).

Think of Paul writing those encouraging words from a bleak prison cell! A *prison cell*. And yet he continued to press on. Paul continued to follow God's call. He strove to forget the past. He kept his head up and his hope alive. And if Paul can do it (from a *prison cell*), we can too.

Maybe you didn't ask for a new beginning. Maybe you're struggling with the loss of a loved one or the loss of a relationship or job. Maybe you've left the town where so many memories reside. Or maybe you can't embrace your new beginning because the past keeps resurfacing. Past hang-ups. Past regrets. Past strongholds.

So often we forget God knows our struggles and the baggage we carry. We must bring it to Him and say, "God, I can't keep dwelling on the past. Forgive me for the wrongs I've done and renew my mind, Lord. Let me accept this clean slate You've so graciously given me.

Give me the strength to press on and receive the new things You want to do in my life."

We can't do anything about the past, so what's the point of dwelling on it? Revisiting the mistakes of yesterday only hardens our hearts and makes us angry and bitter. It puts up a wall that prohibits God from using us to our full potential. Living in the past forbids us from claiming the new beginning God wants to give us. No, we are to obey the Word and forget former things—we are to strive forward (Philippians 3:13). We aren't instructed to let our past define us, but rather we are to welcome new beginnings (no matter how intimidating they may seem).

We are to go when He sends us, whether that is spiritually, emotionally, or physically.

Because God promises us He has a good plan for our future—a plan to prosper us and give us hope (Jeremiah 29:11), we must trust He will do what He says. We must say, "Holla!" to yesterday and say, "How you doin'?" to the present.

One day my children will move from their hometown, the same way I did when I went to college. Even as I cry and fall down in the driveway and hold on to their ankles and beg them not to leave, they'll still have to go if God sends them. And they'll take those memories of bugs in a jar and the sound of bullfrogs on a summer night with them. They'll carry a little piece of their hometown with them wherever they go. They'll carry all the pieces of the puzzle.

But, still, they must go. They must do a new thing.

The time comes when we all must go. When we all must do a new thing.

Instead of being fearful of new beginnings, we must embrace the changes God places in our lives. He gives us a beautiful opportunity to bloom where we're planted. He has a plan, and it is good.

CHAPTER 6

Arise and Call Yourself Blessed

In the early 1980s, Cabbage Patch Kids were all the rage, and I was a mama to four of them: Kirk, Lisa, Alexis, and Brantley. I changed their outfits daily and brushed their yarn hair. When they were naughty, I gently popped them on their little butts where the "Xavier Roberts" tattoo was printed. They meant the world to me, those dolls. I tucked them into bed with me every night and made sure they had toys available to them while I went to school each day. I put them in their Sunday best and strapped them tightly into the back of my mother's Oldsmobile on our way to church.

I have always been maternal. When I was just a kid, I pictured having a house full of kids. I wanted to be a stay-at-home mother just like my own mama. I wanted to pack lunches for school, buy cute little clothes, bandage boo-boos, and cheer from the bleachers. For as long as I can remember, I always wanted to be a mother.

My first pregnancy was not fun. I was not one of those glowing pregnant women with a perfect baby bump, thick hair, and healthy nails. No. I was a huge, waddling duck with all-day sickness, back pain, and terrible acne. One afternoon I caught a glimpse of my arm in my car's side mirror. I had a bat wing. A legit bat wing. I had fifteen pounds of dangling fat hanging from my upper arm, so I whipped into a drive-through, ate a bacon cheeseburger, and tried to forget about it.

Because of preeclampsia, I was induced a week before my due date. And despite the agony of having my water broken with what looked like the hickory switch my grandmother used to spank me when I talked back to her, it was the most beautiful miracle I'd ever experienced. It was far better than front-row Pearl Jam tickets or winning that poetry contest in high school or the day my daddy announced we were getting a pool.

When I held that little bundle in a pastel pink blanket, I was overcome with joy. My dream had finally come true. I was a mother.

Not long after my Natalie Ann was born, the nurse brought her into the hospital room. As Jason slept on the uncomfortable chair in the corner, we had our first moment alone. She quietly gazed up at me with the most beautiful blue eyes. She wouldn't break her stare, and I wouldn't dare break mine. I stroked her fuzzy head and prayed over her. I prayed for her future and asked God to let me be the perfect mother to her. I thanked Him for this blessing. I thanked Him she didn't have yarn hair like my Cabbage Patch dolls. It was the most special moment I'd ever experienced because I knew right then my life had changed for the better.

I happily quit my secretarial job to stay home with my daughter. She was such a good baby she even slept through the night from birth. We spent the days cuddling on the couch and watching Baby Einstein videos (the reason she's in gifted classes today). Lord have mercy, she was so perfect, and I wanted ten more just like her.

I wanted ten more *girls* just like her because I discovered I loved being a mother to a daughter. I loved the bond and the bows. Kirk, my Cabbage Patch son in overalls, was a fine young man, but I didn't want any "real" boys. Being a mother to a house full of girls was the new desire of my heart.

And so, I started praying for that. "God, give me more little girls! Give me more girls, God! I want some more girls!"

In December 2009, Natalie was at Mother's Day Out at First Methodist (sweetly sharing toys with her friends because she was the perfect toddler, remember?), and

I was on a table in my obstetrician's office. Jason stood beside me and we both eagerly watched the monitor as the nurse put cold gel on my large stomach.

The little blob on the screen was a girl. I already knew. How did I know? Because that's what I'd prayed for countless times. Because my desire was God-given. Because I wanted to dress the little blob and Natalie Ann in matching outfits. Because I wanted to name the baby after my mother. Because I was destined to be a mother to daughters.

The nurse began typing on the keyboard and three little words appeared on the screen hanging over my large stomach:

IT'S A BOY!

Jason's eyes lit up as he exhaled joyfully. A boy! A boy to catch the football, to dress in camo and join him in the deer stand. A boy to talk to about carburetors and wrenches and spark plugs. He was getting a boy, and he was ecstatic.

I grinned at the words on the screen, but I will admit to you my heart sank. I'm still ashamed to say it, and as vile as it sounds, I did not want a son. I didn't know how to be a mother to a boy. I wouldn't possibly have the same sweet bond with a boy as I did with Natalie Ann. I didn't want a nursery decorated in primary colors and choo-choo trains. I didn't want to buy overalls that looked like Kirk's.

I was sorely disappointed.

I managed to smile and put on an Oscar-winning performance that I was excited to bear a boy, but I was really confused and even somewhat devastated and deceived by my intuition, perhaps deceived by God. Hadn't God heard my prayers? Didn't He know I wanted another girl? Wasn't He supposed to grant the desires of my heart? What was I going to do with all of Natalie's infant hairbows and dresses I'd saved?

I know it sounds ridiculous to be upset over a child's gender, but I was, and the distress sent me into a depression. I was low and vulnerable, and not only that, I was physically sick for most of the pregnancy. My doctor chalked both the emotional and physical sickness up to hormones, but I knew something more was happening. I lacked joy and peace.

So, the Enemy did what he does best—he took advantage of my distraught and vulnerable state and started putting despicable thoughts in my mind.

You won't love this boy.

I heard that horrible sentence in my head relentlessly. I heard it as I folded laundry, as I washed dishes, as I stared at my precious little girl, as I reluctantly purchased ball caps and dinosaur onesies.

You won't love your own son. You are such a horrible mother.

Repeat times 1,200,999,292.

As if the thought I wouldn't love the child in my womb wasn't horrific and depressing enough, I was plagued with new disturbing thoughts of chaos and confusion. The new thoughts didn't attack my ability to love a son but instead attacked my faith.

God failed you, Susannah. He knew you wanted a little girl. He knew the desires of your heart, but He failed you. He doesn't care about you.

What in the world? What in the ever-loving world was happening to my mind? Why was I being tormented like this? What was this vicious attack on my thought life?

I cried out to God for help, for restoration, and for the first time in my life, I wasn't sure He was there. I couldn't hear His wisdom. When I prayed I felt as if I was just speaking into thin air. I was terrified when I cried out to Him but could not feel His presence.

He's abandoned you. He doesn't care about you.

I vividly remember locking myself in the bathroom one night while Jason and Natalie slept. I slid my heavy, pregnant body to the cold tile floor, and as my bat wings flapped, I ugly sobbed. I had so much snot covering my face, I looked like a newly hatched Gremlin. I begged God to rescue me from the thoughts running through my mind. I begged Him to fill my heart with love for the little boy in my womb. I begged Him to strengthen my faith. I begged Him for help.

Instead of being blanketed in peace when I prayed, as I usually was, I heard, *Who are you praying to? You've been a fool all these years to believe in your God. He doesn't even exist. If He did, He would have freed you by now. He would have comforted you by now.*

Over and over I thought it.

He doesn't exist.

Every hour. Every day. Relentlessly. Repeatedly.

He doesn't exist.

Worn and weary, I read scriptures I'd read a hundred times, and they no longer made sense to me. I started to question what I was reading. I started to believe possibly God wasn't real—and if He was, He truly had abandoned me.

And it all started the moment I learned I was going to have a son.

Ephesians 6:12 tells us our struggle isn't merely against flesh and blood. We wrestle against dark and wicked spiritual forces. The Enemy was dumping lies and garbage into my thought life, and because I didn't know the first thing about putting on the full armor of God (Ephesians 6:10–18), I believed his crap. I truly believed I wasn't going to love the boy in my womb. I believed we were going to go through life resenting one another, and I drowned in guilt over it. I believed I was abandoned by a God who may or may not even be real.

See? This is what the Enemy does. He seeks to kill, steal, and destroy. He seeks to rob us of peace and joy. He seeks to throw us into a state of darkness and despair and leave us there.

But, let me tell you, the moment I locked eyes with

my newborn son, Bennett, I immediately felt the Lord's presence and comfort wash over me. For the first time in months, I knew without a doubt my God, my Savior, my Comforter was right there with me. He was just as present as my husband, my mama, and the doctor. He was just as present as the precious boy I held in my arms. I now like to say I was delivered the moment I delivered!

Bennett wasn't wrapped in a pink blanket or wearing a bow, but I could not have loved that child more. I knew right then all of those debilitating thoughts had been vicious lies. I knew God had given me a son for a great purpose. I knew because the Lord spoke a revelation to me, right there in the hospital room, as I stroked my baby's head of beautiful dark brown hair and his round peach cheeks while overwhelming joy spilled from my eyes.

You've been attacked because the Enemy wanted you to renounce Me. *The Enemy wanted to separate you from* Me *in hopes you wouldn't raise this boy—both your children—on* My *Word. Because this child was a threat to the Enemy before he was even born.*

Wow. Wow. Wow.

Suddenly it all made sense. Oh, it all made so much sense! All the darkness and the despair and the spiritual warfare finally made sense. Satan knew if he could convince me to believe his lies—God doesn't exist and the Bible is a storybook—I would not raise my son on the

Word. I would not raise my son on the truth. The Enemy was scared to death of my baby boy while he was still in my womb and was doing all he could to disrupt my son's inheritance. Because Jeremiah 1:5 says God knew us before He formed us in the womb and He set us apart!

I also understood why the Lord allowed me to endure the trial, why He stayed quiet through the storm: because He knew it would mature me spiritually. He knew it would teach me not to rely on my thoughts and feelings or every lie that runs through my head, but instead on the infallible Word of God.

God knew the struggle, and finally the sweet revelation, would make me realize just how significant my role is as a mother. And possibly help *you* realize just how significant *your* role is to a child—as a mother or a sister or an aunt.

The Enemy cowers at our children, and we cannot take that lightly. If we care for children in our lives, we have been given them to love, to nurture, to protect, to dress in precious outfits, yes, but we must also mold them to do great work for the kingdom. It's imperative we pray diligently over them and send them into the world armed with the knowledge found in the Word of God. It's vital we refute the lies the Enemy speaks to us about our children, our heritage from the Lord, and instead speak words of life and victory over them! It's imperative we prepare these soldiers of God's army—to sow into them the Scriptures. It's our responsibility to help our babies discern the great voice of truth in all the voices coming at them.

In Matthew 9:37 Jesus said to His disciples, "The harvest is plentiful but the workers are few." Jesus looked out upon the people and said, "Look at the potential here! This is a harvest of souls! Who is going to witness to them and tell them the good news? Who is going to step up and do the work? Who is going to sow the seed? Who is going to be a laborer instead of a loiterer?"

Mamas, our children are our field. They are ready for us, as their mothers, to sow some substantial, life-changing, fruit-bearing seeds into them because the world isn't going to do it. Kids in the hallways aren't going to tell your children they are loved and accepted and perfect in Christ. The world isn't going to tell them they have victory over the fiery darts of the Enemy. The world isn't going to sow seeds of love and encouragement and witness and righteous testimony into them. In fact, the Enemy and this world will try to kill the field, steal the seeds, and destroy the harvest.

You have to be the diligent farmer in your children's lives. You have to sow spiritual seeds and then, praise God, watch a sprout bloom within them—a sprout in the form of the Holy Spirit and the fruits of the Spirit: love, joy, peace, patience, kindness, goodness, faithfulness, gentleness, and self-control (Galatians 5:22–23).

That's the harvest.

I pray you recognize what a precious, precious gift

motherhood is. I pray you realize it truly is a God-ordained calling. I pray you realize it is a monumental commission to be entrusted with these soldiers of God's army—these soldiers who threaten the Enemy. I pray you see the work to be done and the seeds to be sown.

I pray you recognize it. I pray you receive it. I pray you relish in it.

And arise and call yourself blessed.

CHAPTER 7

The Upside to Life's Downs

It was November 22, 1992. My father had been sober for a little over a year, but on Saturday, November 21, 1992, he fell off the wagon—and it was a pretty hard fall. He didn't come home after playing a round of golf that afternoon, and my mother and I were both worried he was tying one on. When he finally phoned her hours later, his words were slurred, and our greatest fear became reality. I'll never forget watching my mother in her bathrobe, standing by her bed screaming into the cordless phone, "Not again, Billy Brown! We won't go through this again!"

Mama chain-smoked and paced the house while I worried because my daddy was drunk again. He was in a camp house on the river with a group of friends, strumming the guitar and playing cards while the whiskey flowed like water. I feared Mama was going to leave him this time. I'd be a child of divorce. When would I even see my father? He'd be drinking on the weekends and wouldn't have time for me, but Mama wasn't going to spend another thirteen years waiting on that man to stumble in at 2:00 a.m., scorch his supper in the microwave, and pass out on the couch. Her own father was an alcoholic, and she refused to keep going through what her own sweet mother went through.

I spent the night in my mother's bed, my eyes swollen from the tears and my stomach hurting from the stress. She was on the phone half the night venting to her best friend and my sister who was away at college. I remember her lengthy prayer that night as she held me close to her side. I remember her praying he'd safely get home down the curvy river road. I remember her praying for his conviction. I also remember her praying we'd never go through this again.

And her prayers were answered.

My mother was the pianist in our country Baptist church, so she could not miss services the next morning, but she allowed me to play hooky. I mean, my dad had just fallen off the wagon and I'd spent the entire night crying. I really didn't want to put on one of my Simplicity pattern dresses and do a craft in Sunday school. So I cuddled up in the bed with my Lhasa Apso, Peaches, and watched George Bailey run down the streets of Bedford Falls.

My thoughts were consumed by my father. When he had come in the night before, he did not bother coming into my mother's bedroom to speak to us. He knew he was in trouble and the best thing for him would be to sleep on the couch. Although he'd been out partying all night, he still managed to get up early that Sunday morning and go play golf. So I had not seen him yet, but I assumed we'd have a family meeting later that afternoon. That made me nervous and uneasy.

As George Bailey ran down the black-and-white streets, I heard the squeaky kitchen door open and close. Soon I saw my tall, thin, handsome daddy pass the bedroom door and continue down the hall. When he didn't speak to me, I got up to investigate. And there I saw him lying on the floor and moaning in pain.

What a hangover, I thought.

I called out to him several times, but he wouldn't reply. Finally, he pushed himself up and walked toward me. He only made it a few steps, though, before he fell again.

I remembered the old folks at church describing a heart attack like "an elephant sitting on your chest." Because my father was clutching at his heart and moaning in pain, I knew this must be the problem instead of a hangover, but it just didn't seem right. My daddy didn't fit the description for heart-attack victims. He was only forty-two years old. Yeah, he was a drinker and there was a Vantage cigarette hanging from his lips nearly every waking minute, but heart attacks were for grandfathers and people who ate meat for dessert. It just didn't make sense to my eleven-year-old mind.

While my dog curled next to him on the floor, I ran to the kitchen telephone and dialed 911. I told the operator my father was sick and needed help immediately. Then I dialed the church and told Mrs. Betty to send my mother home. Once the phone calls had been made, I paced the blue floral house, for the first time in my life knowing true terror and anxiety. I'll never forget Peaches resting close to him, as if she knew something terrible was happening. Her head was down and her brown eyes shifted about the house. I realized at that moment just how intuitive animals are.

When it was too much for my young mind to comprehend, for my swollen, tear-soaked eyes to see, I scooped the saddened dog into my arms and ran outside. Freezing in nothing but Garfield pajamas, I pushed the golf clubs, Beatles tapes, and crumpled packs of cigarettes out of the way and climbed into my daddy's Chevrolet. There my devoted dog and I waited for the ambulance to arrive.

The paramedics finally came, and only a few seconds later, my mother's Oldsmobile screeched into the driveway as if a stunt driver were behind the wheel. Frazzled, Mama ran into the house and her best friend, Mrs. Murphy, stayed in the driveway to console me.

Soon my father was wheeled out of our living room on a stretcher, and my mom climbed into the ambulance with him and left me with Mrs. Murphy and the depressed dog.

I sat on that floral nightmare of a couch and waited on the call from my mother—the call that would explain that this was just indigestion or the flu or something mundane. I waited for her to call and say this was, indeed, a hangover. This was my dad's first hangover— long overdue after not drinking for so many months. He was going to have a cup of coffee and a piece of toast and smoke a cigarette and come back home. That's exactly what was going to happen. And we were going to cry together as a family. And Daddy would apologize and swear he'd never drink another drop. And then we'd go to Wendy's and I could have a single with cheese and a chocolate Frosty. Yep. That's what was going to happen any minute now. The call was coming. I would hear her comforting voice over the line. Mama would ease my fears. Mama would call and crack one of her hilarious jokes that deserved a rim shot.

But that call never came.

Instead, an EMT walked through my front door, without knocking. This man, tall, heavy, and bald, waltzed through my blue living room and told my mother's friend he was there to retrieve the resuscitating equipment left on the stupid blue carpet. Mrs. Murphy held me close to her side and asked the man how my father was doing.

Extremely casually, too casually, the bald man answered, "He didn't make it."

That man, that stranger, whose face I can still see so clearly twenty-six years later, spoke the words that pierced my innocent heart and robbed me of my child-like joy. We'd had ups and downs in my family, but for the most part, I thought of us as the stars of a sitcom with jokes constantly flowing or humorous events taking place. Now I felt like I had a starring role in a catastrophic drama. I was on an after-school special. I was utterly and hopelessly broken.

My father's funeral was one of the largest our town had seen because everyone knew him—and not because he was an alcoholic. He was known for his kindness and willingness to give the shirt off his back. He was known for being positive and jolly no matter what demons he secretly battled. My daddy was just an all-around great, funny guy, and his death was a loss not only to our family but to his coworkers, golf partners, and many friends.

My mother, the young widow, left with heavy burdens and responsibilities, came home from the funeral home that cold November afternoon, her face soaked with tears and her heart shattered. But she was determined to find praise in the storm. She was determined to speak Scripture over the loss we'd endured that day: he'd "prefer to be away from the body and at home with the Lord" (2 Corinthians 5:8). Mama was confident, despite my father's sins, that he'd been saved by amazing grace a few years before while on a business trip. Therefore, she was confident he'd finally arrived in the place where his soul and all of our souls long to be. My daddy was home—his heavenly home. He no longer battled addiction to alcohol. He no longer battled guilt for choosing golf outings over family outings. My daddy no longer battled. Was that anything to mourn?

It would be a lie to say that waves of grief didn't pelt us all to the sand and leave us feeling as if we were drowning. No, the grief came. It came often at first, and so many years later, it still comes. The waves are smaller, but they still come. I haven't seen my daddy in decades, but I still long for his hugs and his jokes and the sound of his raspy voice. When I feel despair creeping in, I cling to Scriptures and faith that the Lord is near to the brokenhearted and our present sufferings are nothing compared to eternal glory. I cling to the happiness found in humor. I cling to the wonderful memories of my childhood sitcom. Those are the moments that I choose to turn my tears into laughter. That's what sees me through.

The Bible says we will have trials and tribulations in this world. We are going to experience storms and valleys, and we may even find ourselves questioning why God has allowed things to happen and whether He really is good. Oh, the Enemy loves this. He loves to creep into our thoughts, especially when we are downtrodden and vulnerable, and whisper to us that God has forsaken us. He doesn't want us to see the beauty in the ashes. He wants us to question God's love and mercy. He wants us to feel like victims. And he definitely wants us to suffer a bout of amnesia and forget all the times in the past when God pulled us through.

When I begin to question God's goodness, when I begin to question why things weren't different—why my daddy had to have a heart attack while I was home alone, or why he had to die when my mother and I were both angry with him for drinking—I have to cling to the Word and remember that *all* things work together for good for those who love Him. I have to remember God is the Author of my life's story and every tragedy I've gone through has been His perfect will. I have to remember that there's beautiful purpose to be found in pain.

I also remind myself of the incredible pain Jesus endured on that old, rugged cross. Mercy! He was bloodied and beaten and battered. He was ridiculed and mocked. He endured pain we cannot even comprehend. But, wasn't the beautiful purpose revealed? Wasn't it revealed three days later when the tomb proved empty? Praise hands!

We cannot measure God's goodness solely on our emotions and experience. Instead, we have to know—truly know—that our Father bestows perfect gifts on us that our mere minds cannot even comprehend. Whatever our trial, no matter how painful or debilitating, it can be considered a gift if it points us to Jesus.

That is the upside to life's downs.

CHAPTER 8

Hang Up Those Hang-Ups

I love to eat. Do you hear me? I *love* to eat. Like, I get really excited about eating. You know how kids react when their parents tell them they are going to Disney? I'm that way when my husband says, "We're going out for steak."

My love of food is no doubt attributed to the fact that my mother was a phenomenal cook. She was like a Southern Julia Child, which means she was like a crazy cross between Paula Deen and Lucy Buffett.

Mama knew how to whip up homemade biscuits and potatoes in a hot, buttery way for every single meal. Meat, potatoes, bread. Meat, potatoes, bread. For my entire childhood. Carbs are absolutely delicious, but they are absolute hades on a waistline. So it's no surprise that I was a chunky kid.

I once went on a camping trip with my friend and her family, and her brother found my extremely large bathing suit inside our tent. Because I hadn't worn it yet, no one knew it was my suit, so I made fun of it with them. "Ha! That thing is huge!" My friend's brother assumed it was his stepmom's bathing suit, but now that I look back on it, I don't know why they thought their stepmother would have a bathing suit with a unicorn on it.

I had to swim in a T-shirt and shorts all weekend to hide that the suit was really mine. I think I left that unicorn suit at the campsite because I didn't want anyone to see me pack it in my bag. Ten bucks of my mother's money left in a pile of pine needles . . .

I haven't been overweight in years thanks in part to watching some Netflix specials on how we are what we eat. I now only buy organic meat and produce, and I don't devour corn dogs like they are potato chips or pour high-fructose corn syrup down my throat at every meal. I used to scoff at the ladies in the grocery store wearing their workout clothes while pushing a shopping cart containing overpriced organic strawberries and whole wheat taco shells, but I've realized they had it right all along because our bodies aren't garbage cans and we need to stop filling them with junk. And although I still love bad foods, I make better choices, and let me tell you, it's nice to go for a brisk walk and not sweat bacon bits.

Based on my love affair with food, it's probably obvious that I have an addictive personality. The first time I smoked a cigarette in my friend's car when I was fifteen, I was a slave to tobacco. I was that stupid kid who lit one up every day I pulled onto the main road from the high school parking lot and then doused my car with aerosol air freshener that left everything smelling like a bouquet of formaldehyde. And there was a wild stint in my late teens and early twenties when I drank so much alcohol that my "check liver" light was constantly on.

And I come from a long line of addicts.

My daddy, a functioning alcoholic, went to the country club every day after work to play golf and drink whiskey until well after my bedtime. Some nights I would wake to the sound of him stumbling around the kitchen and warming up his dinner. Have you ever heard a drunk person operating a microwave? He pressed so many buttons it sounded like he was launching a space shuttle. And, unfortunately, his button-pressing resulted in a scorched plate of meat, bread, and potatoes. I would roll over and go back to sleep because I thought it was normal for daddies not to come home right after work.

Recently I listened to some cassette tapes of my father and his friends singing and playing guitar in our living room. In the background, I hear beer cans slamming onto the coffee table or being tossed into the garbage. And occasionally, I hear me, at five or six, asking Daddy for a Flintstone Push-Up or another Little Debbie. As a child, it seemed completely normal for the sounds of Led Zeppelin and the Eagles to blare from my living room every weekend as I stepped over empty cans and bottles.

Both of my grandfathers were alcoholics too. Hilliard would run off on a two- or three-day bender and leave my sweet grandmother at home with two little girls. Billy always had a smell about him that I thought was cologne until the first time I got a whiff of Southern Comfort and put two and two together. So I knew that the generational curse of alcoholism ran in my family.

When I was ten, I read my daddy a letter I'd written about how I didn't want him to drink anymore because he was never home. I wrote about the time he picked me up from the babysitter's and weaved all over the road. I wrote about the time he and my mother got into a drunken argument in front of all of my friends at my slumber party. And as I read it to him, it was the second time I'd ever seen my father cry. Without hesitation, my daddy agreed to go to rehab because he didn't want to hurt me anymore.

When he got out a month later, our family seemed normal. If he wasn't home after work, he was at an AA meeting. For the first time in my ten years of life, we went on family outings. We went to the zoo and matinees. While on vacation, he didn't leave my mother and siblings and me on the beach while he went back to the hotel balcony or some bayside bar to drink. That lasted for a little over a year until the night my father fell off the wagon.

All the dysfunction associated with my daddy's addiction didn't stop me from drinking. I scored a fake ID in the eleventh grade and spent nearly every weekend parked on some field road with a group of friends, downing a six-pack and listening to Alice in Chains. I would drink until I passed out or threw up, and then I would drive myself home. I know the only reason I made it home alive many nights was because of my mother's prayers.

When I was in college, I was still drinking quite heavily. Instead of just drinking on the weekend, though, I found a reason to go out two or three times a week. One evening, while driving back to my friend's house, I saw blue lights in my rearview mirror. When the police officer asked me to walk a straight line, I looked at him and said, "There's no possible way. Book me, Danno." And he did. And I spent my first night in jail.

I sat in that drunk tank for hours praying and wondering where I'd gone wrong. I thought about the heartache my father's drinking had caused not only me but my poor mother, and now I was putting her through it all again. After a friend bailed me out of jail that night, I went to my mother's house and had never been so scared or ashamed to tell her where I'd been. I think dragon's fire shot out of her mouth as she scolded me, and I straightened myself up for a little while. But, the next year I got another DUI. I lost my license for twelve months and had to depend on rides from friends to get to and from work and college.

I'm embarrassed just typing that.

I was dating Jason at the time, and he, too, was a partier. We spent our weekends drunk and screaming at each other. I liked to throw things, and the walls of Jason's poor house proved it. It's amazing the damage an ashtray can do to Sheetrock. And one night I got so mad at him I left him at the bar and walked home through the not-so-safest part of town. Again, I had a mother who prayed constantly over me, and that's the only reason I didn't end up dead in a ditch.

I drank heavily up until the moment I learned I was pregnant with Natalie Ann, and when she was born, something in me changed. I was a mother, and I no longer had the desire to stay out all night and throw ashtrays. And I certainly didn't want to be the kind of parent my father was to me. I shuddered at the very thought of my children sitting across from me in a chair and reading me a letter begging me to get help.

But not only did having a child change me, *the Holy Spirit did*.

I'd been saved when I was in elementary school. I was raised in church and prayed and asked God for forgiveness when the hangover had me hugging the toilet or when I was sitting on a concrete bench in a jail cell. I knew I wasn't living for the Lord, and I was convicted of it, but I continued down a destructive path. But when I started really praying for Jesus to remove the temptations from my heart, He did it. The Holy Spirit came in and changed both me and Jason. And trust me, the fact that my beer-loving, karaoke-singing, pool-shooting husband no longer drinks is nothing short of a miracle straight from God. And look at me: the stupid young girl who was once puking Boone's Farm in a cotton field now writes devotionals.

We really can do *all* things through Christ who strengthens us. First Corinthians 10:13 says, "No temptation has overtaken you that is not common to man. God is faithful, and he will not let you be tempted beyond your ability, but with the temptation he will also provide the way of escape, that you may be able to endure it" (ESV). God will help us hang up those hang-ups!

Hang-ups don't have to be addictions to food or nicotine or alcohol like mine. Temptations can present themselves to us in many different ways. We can be tempted to constantly fear and worry. And, the Enemy wants us to be bound to strongholds. He wants us so tightened by his grip that we cannot see our purpose— that we cannot clearly hear from the Lord and live an abundant life of peace.

According to Luke 10:17–19, we have a way out. We have authority. We have authority to tread all over the power of the Enemy.

"The seventy-two returned with joy and said, 'Lord, even the demons submit to us in your name.' He said to them, 'I saw Satan fall like lightning from heaven. I have given you authority to trample on snakes and scorpions and to overcome all the power of the enemy; nothing will harm you.'"

You hear that? We can tread all over snakes and scorpions. Although I don't recommend you intentionally stepping on a snake or scorpion in cheap flip-flops.

But believing we're always going to be in oppression to our hang-ups is a lie straight from hell. Believing we are just naturally worried, anxious people is a lie straight from hell. Believing we need alcohol or drugs or whatever vice to survive is a lie straight from hell. Believing depression isn't curable is a lie straight from hell.

God's sweet truth found in the Bible sets us free. The sweet truth of Scripture causes the Enemy to cower. The sweet truth that Jesus died on the cross for every iniquity, every weakness, every sin sets us free. We've got to know the truth, meditate on the truth, and keep the truth bound around our necks and in our hearts.

God also provides relief to us through antidepressants, therapy, rehab, seeing a Christian counselor, and many other solutions. These things *are not* substitutes for the Word—the truth—but they are wonderful tools to help defeat our strongholds. I'm proof that prayer works. And Lexapro ain't bad either.

Refuse to believe that strongholds are just a way of life for you and your loved ones. That right there is one of those lies straight from hell.

The truth. The truth. The truth.

Know it. Claim it. Speak it.

CHAPTER 9

Leave the Trolls Under the Bridge

Natalie Ann is a middle schooler now, and she and her friends all wear cute sweaters and leggings and Birkenstocks. They put their hair into fishtail braids and messy buns and finish off their shabby-chic look with pearl earrings. When she walks into school every morning, she looks like she stepped right out of a Gap ad.

But when I was my daughter's age, I was twice as wide as I was tall. My feet were huge (my loafers looked more like bread loaves), and my White Rain–doused bangs were in the shape of a large-barrel curling iron. For some godforsaken reason, I thought it was a good idea to tuck my T-shirts into my Duck Head shorts even though my butt was as flat as the pancake centerfold in an IHOP menu. Needless to say, middle school was a really awkward and difficult time for me.

My awkwardness did not go unnoticed by a group of popular girls and their minion boyfriends. They made it their mission every day to oink at me when I passed them in the hallway, or tell me I should be drinking low-fat milk at lunchtime, or do the old "cover their mouth and whisper to each other and then point and laugh at me" trick. I know as Christians, we aren't supposed to hate others, but gosh I hated them. I really, really, *really* hated them.

My mother wasn't having any of it. Against my wishes, she called the bullies' parents and gave them a piece of her mind. They defended their girls and denied their precious children would ever ridicule a schoolmate. My protective mama tried to help, but her involvement only fueled the girls' fire to make my life living hell for two years. Now I was not only "fat," but I was a "fat mama's baby."

When I'd come home depressed, Mama would pray over me, "No weapon formed against you shall prosper." She continually told me how "fearfully and wonderfully" made I was, as I loosened my woven belt and dropped another dollop of mashed potatoes on my plate. Along with my mother's powerful, Spirit-filled prayers, I also had some really supportive friends who cheered me up when those older girls made fun of me. Middle school was a rough time, but I got through it, and eventually the girls grew bored with insulting me and moved on.

Side note: One of those bullies recently sent me a friend request on Facebook. We are instructed to love and forgive our enemies, yes, but nowhere in the Bible does it say we have to be friends with them on social media. I've never denied a request so quickly in my life.

Anyway, the summer before my freshman year, a miracle occurred. I sprouted up about fourteen feet. And when I shot up tall like my father, the fat stretched vertically. Presto! For the first time in my life, I was thin, and all of that extra fat made for something to put in my training bra. When I walked into high school for the first time, feeling confident, I was approached by a group of boys I'd known my entire life.

"Susannah, we thought you were a new girl. You aren't fat anymore!"

I retorted with, "No, I'm not new. But I see all of those zits on your face are."

That confidence was short-lived because those boys found a new reason to tease me. They made fun of my height. Lord, it was annoying. For two years, I constantly heard from a group of them, "How's the air up there? How's the air up there?" I slouched my shoulders and dashed into class and wished I was petite and could wear cute wedges that wouldn't cause me to hit my head on lighting fixtures. Those boys really did a number to my self-esteem.

One of those same boys asked me out a few years later and I told him, "I'm sorry. I couldn't hear you from way up here."

When I became an adult, I thought my days of being bullied were over, PTL. But, as my social media following grew, I realized pretty quickly that wasn't the case. When you reach over a million people online, you're bound to interact with some real miserable grouches who want to tear down anyone they can. I can't even tell you how many nasty emails, messages, and comments I've received. Lord have mercy, I've had people criticize everything from my hair to my accent to my faith to how I raise my children. I've been told to die, shut up, and die again. I've been told I'm ignorant, closed-minded, and annoying. I've been told I'm a horrible writer, a horrible wife, I'm not funny, and I should do something about my eyebrows. (I couldn't really disagree with that one. It had been a few months since my last waxing when I got that comment.) I've even been told that I use too many adjectives when I write! Someone really hated me because I use adjectives! For the love! I replied with, "Please kiss my fat, wide, round, cellulite-covered, lily-white . . ." I've been told my earrings are tacky, my eyeliner is crooked, my boobs are too small, my videos are too long, and even that I have ugly dogs. Listen, you can talk about my breast size all day long, but I'll cut someone for talking about my dogs.

I was doing a live video one day and telling a story about buying tall-length pants from China on eBay. Listen, tall-length pants in China are not the same as tall-length pants in America. I tried them on and they resembled the pleated culottes my chaperone, Mrs. Lee, used to wear to swim in at church camp. My entire calf was exposed.

As I was telling this tale, a real-time comment popped up from a girl asking, "Who is this moron? Is she on drugs?" I tried to ignore the words on the screen and continue to tell my story, but I started to doubt myself. *Why does she think I'm a moron? Do people agree with her? Do I sound like a moron? Why does she think I'm on drugs? I don't look like I'm on drugs, do I? Are my pupils dilated? Why would she say that? Because I'm rambling about China pants? Do you have to be on drugs to ramble about China pants on the internet?* And then she commented again. And again. Didn't this person know I could see what she was saying about me? Why was she taking a dig at me? I was just trying to bring a little laughter to the world at the expense of a bad eBay purchase.

She kept on berating me, and somehow, I morphed from a moron to a "backwoods Bible-toting hillbilly." My faithful viewers came to my defense and told this heckler to quit watching if she found me so annoying. Which makes sense, doesn't it? When I'm annoyed by something, I take the "flight" approach. This person obviously took the "fight" approach. I mean, I'm not the biggest fan of the Kardashians, so I simply change the channel when they come on instead of banging out a twelve-page letter criticizing their life choices and sending it to them via overnight mail.

And yet, she kept on. I couldn't take any more of her insults. I told her to go back to whatever bridge underbelly she came from and clicked on her name and blocked her from the video. Sometimes, that's exactly what we have to do. We don't have to be susceptible to those who find so many faults with us. If you have someone in your life who is constantly bringing you down, block, delete, and repeat if necessary. You don't need someone dumping all of their insecurities and hurts onto you.

When I read nasty comments like those, I suddenly feel like that chubby middle schooler or that awkwardly tall high schooler again. I am consumed by doubt over an insult made by an iPhone-toting coward. And the Devil loves that. Oh, he loves it because he wants us to be uncomfortable in our own skin. He wants us blind to our worth and blind to how much Jesus loves us. He wants us heartbroken and worried and struggling with low self-esteem. He loves it when we base our self-worth on what some bully says about us, because the Devil is the biggest bully of all.

This is just another reason it is so important to get the truth found in Scripture into our hearts (and our children's hearts). The Enemy will use someone degrading us as the perfect opportunity to bring us down, but we can't let him. Nope. We've got to tell him to shut up. We've got to replace his lies with truth. We have to replace his invectives with what God, the Creator of the universe, says about us.

Hey, guess what, ya big bully?

I am a child of God. I am a branch of the true Vine. I am a friend of Jesus. I am forgiven. I am accepted by Christ. Through Christ, I have wisdom and redemption. My body is a temple of the Holy Spirit who dwells in me. I am chosen. I am holy. I am blameless. I am meant to produce good works. I am an heir of Christ's promises. I am precious. I am wonderfully made. I am a conqueror. I am special. I am beautiful. God supplies my needs. God loves me. God chose me. God accepts me. God made me in His perfect image. And God made some really cute dogs just for me too.

And the more we embrace the beautiful truths found in the Bible about who we really are in Christ, the more stable, grateful, and confident we will be in this world. We can hold our heads up high and know exactly who we are.

Galatians 1:10 says, "Am I now trying to win the approval of human beings, or of God? Or am I trying to please people? If I were still trying to please people, I would not be a servant of Christ."

That powerful scripture reminds me that it doesn't matter what everyone else says about me. It doesn't matter if I don't meet someone else's expectations. It doesn't matter that someone thinks I'm a moron on drugs. It doesn't matter that some lady in Des Moines with a puffy-paint cat sweater thinks my nose is too wide. It doesn't matter that some guy hiding behind a computer screen eating Cheetos says my hair looks like broom straw, because I know who I am in Christ. I know what He says about me is so much more important than what this world says about me.

I love, though, on the days when a comment or an email does manage to get me down, that God has a beautiful way of reminding me who I am in Him. A stranger will approach me in a store and smile kindly and say, "I appreciate what you do. You make me laugh, and I just want to thank you for that." He sends an angel, an angel right here on earth shopping in Hobby Lobby in the 50-percent-off wood décor section, to give me encouragement on the days I need it the most.

CHAPTER 10

Don't Wear Them Leggings

A few years ago, during the dead of winter, some friends and I were suffering with a terrible bout of cabin fever. Our children had been forced to stay home from school for several days because there was a thin layer of ice on the road, and the high outside was some absurd number like eight, and the low was an even more absurd number like two. Listen, eight and two don't belong on a weather forecast. Those numbers belong on the scoreboard at an elementary school basketball game.

When the sun finally reappeared and warmed the earth and melted the horrific ice that bound our bored children to our hips for nearly a week, school resumed.

(Praise hands!) My friends and I thought it would be fitting to celebrate with a nice dinner (that didn't consist of canned soup or SpaghettiOs) and to hear a local band perform at a restaurant.

I was really excited to get out for the night. I was beyond ready to trade in the stained sweatpants I'd been wearing all week for a new outfit. I'd seen several *young* ladies wearing leopard-print leggings lately and I thought, *Well, I'm hip. It would probably be a good idea for me to get a pair of those.* Let's just say the first clue I wasn't "hip" was the fact that I used the word *hip*, all right?

So I went to my favorite store and scampered over to unknown territory—the junior department. I didn't care that every young girl in that area of the store assumed I was shopping for my daughter. I quickly found a *snazzy, hip* pair of leopard-print leggings. I paired them with a black tunic and furry boots and then examined my thirty-three-year-old self in the mirror and all I could say was, "RAWR!" I was smoking hot, ladies. Smoking. Hot.

Or so I thought.

I was feeling really good about myself all night as I laughed with my friends and snapped my fingers to the band covering a Bruce Springsteen tune. Never mind I was the only person in the restaurant wearing leopard-print leggings and fuzzy boots. I shrugged it off and conjured my inner Sammy Davis Jr. and told myself those other cats just weren't as hip as me.

The next day, though, a friend posted some online

photos of our night on the town. Right there, front and center, I stuck out like a sore, spotted thumb next to my sisters in their nice jeans and respectable sweaters and billowy scarves. (It's not that standing out is bad—in fact, it's beautiful to be different, but this wasn't a good kind of standing out, all right? Trust me. I was more like a hot, spotted mess that refused to be ignored.) I was mortified as I examined those weird leggings and fuzzy boots, and I realized I looked exactly like a zoo cat. And speaking of zoo cats, I totally could have passed for a cougar too. I'm not talking about the American wildcat (they don't have spots), but I'm referring to the term used to refer to an older woman who preys on a younger man. This would explain why the college-aged waiter was sweating profusely and seemed nervous to make eye contact with me.

Needless to say, as I noticed the leopard print didn't match my crows' feet, I tossed the leggings in a donate pile and decided I was about twenty years too old to shop in the junior department. I mourned that loss for a moment, but I moved on and admitted wearing those leopard-print leggings had been a poor decision.

Yes, worse than the decision to cut my own bangs when I couldn't get an appointment with my hair stylist. Worse than the decision to purchase a fish sandwich from a gas station. Worse than believing a guy who knocked on my door one night and told me a sob story about selling children's books for college tuition and then writing him a two-hundred-dollar check for the Curious George collection only to realize a year later I never received the Curious George collection.

And to top all of that, when I was in high school, I made the poor decision to date a guy who wasn't worth two cents. I knew by the way he'd treated former girl-friends that I shouldn't have anything to do with him because he was a lying, cheating, no-good scoundrel, but his hair was pretty and his truck had loud pipes. So, like a fool, I said yes when he asked me out. Only a few weeks into our relationship, he picked me up to go to the movies with a big purple bruise on his neck. It appeared to be a disgusting hickey, but he was adamant he had been "hurt" while playing basketball. I've heard of people tearing a ligament or spraining an ankle or breaking a bone while playing basketball, but I've never heard of Michael Jordan getting a bruised neck. But, being a fool, I believed him and went to the movies with a boy who had a hickey I hadn't even given him!

I told my mother about his "basketball injury" when I got home that night, and the sigh she let out sounded like a tractor tire leaking air. "Susannah! Baby, are you dumb as a box of rocks?" Apparently, I was.

I've made some really poor decisions in my thirty-seven years, and I'm sure you have too. Many times, we make bad choices simply because we don't consult with the One who matters. Oh, we ask our friends or our parents or our spouse or Yahoo Answers (is that still a thing?) for advice because we love to run to the phone instead of the throne. And if we do consult the Lord, we don't wait for His answer, or we give in to our flesh even when our spirit is screaming *no*! So, we jump in with both feet only to find ourselves in debt or with buyers' remorse or incredibly short bangs.

And many times, we do things simply because we have the right to do them. But having the right to do something doesn't necessarily make it right. Spandex is not a right—it's a privilege. We also have the right to freedom of speech, but we probably shouldn't be cussing out waitresses who accidentally spill our drink or making it our mission to bully every person on social media who has a different opinion. We even have the right to wear leopard-print leggings, but Lord knows it isn't wise.

How it must grieve the Lord when we look in all the wrong places for wisdom and then wonder why everything is going wrong.

We serve a God who cares about every intricate detail of our lives, so we should see what He has to say about our decisions. Maybe there's no proverb that says, "Thou shalt not wear animal prints after the age of thirty," but we can find all of the instructions and solutions in the Good Book.

King Solomon, the author of Proverbs, was Israel's first "celebrity," known for his wisdom and wealth. Even the youth looked up to Solomon solely because he was wise. Not like today. Our kids look up to idiots just because they are popular on Instagram or they have cool tennis shoes or wear "clout goggles" (what in the world?) or know how to drop a sick beat. But Proverbs was actually written primarily for upper-class educated boys. King Solomon wanted to convey to them that a sensible life is one revolving around God, not them.

Proverbs isn't just for upper-class Israeli boys, though. The wisdom found in this book is needed to raise our children, manage our finances, exercise leadership, treat others kindly with our words and deeds, view sex morally, eat and drink healthily, behave as husbands and wives should, control our thoughts, receive correction, deal with offenses, and handle our emotions and attitudes, all of which results in a life of prosperity.

Proverbs is a manual for living.

We oughtn't get knowledge and wisdom confused. Wisdom has nothing to do with how many academic degrees hang on your wall or how many trophies sit on your shelf. I know some "scholars" who are a few cards short of a full deck. Instead, wisdom is the art of competently living in whatever conditions we find ourselves and knowing nothing takes priority over God. Being wise means making choices today that we will be happy with tomorrow (and it means not having to untag yourself in photos of yourself wearing leopard print on social media).

David, King Solomon's father, also said in Psalm 119:66, "Teach me good discernment and knowledge. For I believe in Your commandments" (NASB).

This is our cry. We should be begging the Lord to

teach us and give us wisdom and help us discern which path to take and which choice to make. I should have done that before I agreed to go out with the no-good scoundrel in high school. God probably would have told me to steer clear of him, and I would have argued with God, "But he has pretty hair and loud pipes on his truck." But when God gives us an answer, whether we like it or not, we must obey. It's such sweet surrender when we have faith God will guide our steps and never steer us wrong.

CHAPTER 11

Get in the Game, Mamas

When my daughter came to me, at seven years old, and said, "Mama, I want to play softball!" I cringed a little. Because I was a horrible softball player. I couldn't hit the ball to save my life. I ran away screaming, arms flailing, when the ball traveled toward me at high rates of speed. And listen, sliding on dirt is impossible for a child who met a quota of four corndogs a day. It didn't take long for me to grow tired of the humiliation, give up the game, and sit on the sidelines to watch my friends play. Honestly, I was scared my little girl had inherited my softball abilities and would be humiliated too.

During her first softball game, Natalie Ann proved

to be her mother's daughter. She couldn't catch a ball for squat and she actually turned in a circle when swinging the bat. I was relieved we'd bought a cheap glove instead of a good one, because this wasn't going to last long. Like me, she'd soon get tired of failing and want to pursue something else.

But each week, she was ecstatic to go back to practice. Yes, she kept striking out and the ball never made it into her glove, but she kept going. She refused to just sit in the bleachers and cheer for her friends. She wanted to be on that field, so she kept trying. She went out in the front yard and threw the ball up in the air, and after getting hit in the face a few times, she finally started catching it.

And one day, she hit the ball. Her little legs ran like the dickens and she was finally on first base, her face covered in a smile. To hear me screaming, you'd have thought she'd just nailed a walk-off homerun in World Series Game Seven! I may have teared up a little, and she may have too.

Softball soon became a large part of our lives. Natalie Ann took hitting and pitching lessons every week. I hauled an overloaded wagon packed with bats and coolers and umbrellas and bought things like eye black and Frogg Toggs and portable fans. I took more time picking out the perfect folding chair than I did picking out a couch for our living room. We even splurged on a glove and bat that cost more than my microwave.

One hot afternoon, as I sat in that overpriced, extra-padded folding chair and watched my dusty little girl at second base, I was overcome with admiration. I admired her for having the courage to charge the ball rapidly flying at her instead of screaming, with arms flailing. I admired her for having the courage to get back out there with her head held high and redeem herself after a terrible previous inning. I admired her hard work and determination. I admired her for not just sitting on the sidelines but for playing the game.

The summer of her 8U season, Natalie Ann made the all-star team. Along with twelve other little girls, she spent the majority of her summer vacation on the dirty softball field. Those girls happily sacrificed lazy nights and weekends to practice perfecting their swings and their slides. They pushed through the fatigue of each early morning game, the heat and the sweat and the scorching sun of every afternoon playoff. Twelve little girls were too busy working to complain. Twelve little girls gave their heart and their all on the softball diamond week after week.

It's difficult to accurately put into words the enormous pride that I felt when our all-stars won game after game, championship after championship, proving that their practice and dedication had paid off. As they exited the ball field with sweaty jerseys, stained pants, sandy cleats, and faces covered in smeared eye black and smiles, they knew, we all knew, their team was special.

Parents and grandparents jumped and shouted with

joy as those twelve little girls played undefeated in tournament after tournament. We uploaded countless photos to Facebook declaring our pride for our team as they continued to play their hearts out and seal a spot in the state championship.

All of their hard work came down to a final game at the World Series, and I wasn't about to miss it. Jason and I actually cancelled a trip to New York to watch our daughter stand on the pitching mound that weekend. Tired and worn, though, our all-stars lost the final game by one run in the last inning. Did you hear me? *One run in the last inning!* After so many wins, so many trophies and medals, those little girls finally knew what it was like to lose.

Tears left clean streaks on their dirty faces as they received the second-place trophy. But those tears didn't fall just because they had lost a ball game. Sore losers, they definitely weren't. They cried—and the mamas cried—for a different reason.

They wiped their eyes because the season was over. They knew this team wouldn't play together again. Some of the girls would move up to a different age bracket. They cried because that was the last time they'd assemble on the field in their orange and blue 2015 all-stars jerseys. They cried because they truly loved being together, playing together, winning, and even losing together.

I (poorly) played sports in school, but I never experienced what my young daughter and her teammates experienced that summer. I never formed the kinds of bonds those young ladies formed. They didn't just play ball on some dusty field. They learned some of life's most important lessons.

I watched each girl cheer on her teammates. I watched them pat each other's helmets and tap each other's gloves. I watched them build up one another. When someone struck out or missed a pop fly, I watched them share a bench in a dugout and whisper words of encouragement. I watched them bow down on one knee when a teammate was hurt, as worry covered their faces. I watched those girls love one another. And sometimes those twelve little girls were afraid—afraid of a bigger, better team. Sometimes they were afraid they would lose. But they had faith in one another and played the game anyway because giving up wasn't an option.

Those girls reminded me we are called to encourage and love one another. And when we are called to do the hard things, things that make us afraid, we have to do them anyway.

When I self-published my first book in 2015, I was asked to speak at events. I *loathe* speaking in public, but I did a tri-county tour of libraries and book clubs and talked in detail about plot development, antagonists, and how I found the time to juggle writing and mother-hood. I won't lie. Sometimes I was so nervous about standing in front of a crowd I had to pop half a Xanax and apply a profuse amount of deodorant. I remember pacing backstage at an event and begging the Lord for a hefty dose of courage. I also begged Him not to let me pee my pants or throw up on the podium. And He was faithful to see me through every single speaking engagement.

Then I was called to speak at bigger events. And I wasn't discussing fiction and ideas for sequels. Instead, I was talking to people about Jesus! I spoke to a large group of mothers and impressionable young girls who long to gain this world's (and social media's) approval and who lose sight of what is eternal and everlasting. I spoke to girls who fervently and tirelessly sow seeds into a worldly, unrighteous, secular field and are disappointed time and time again with what they reap—a temporary harvest of approval that soon fades and is replaced by seeds of doubt and low self-esteem and anxiety and fear.

And as I looked out upon those young ladies sitting at beautifully decorated tables in an event hall at a gorgeous antebellum home, I was filled with such immeasurable joy. For the first time, I wasn't nervous to speak. I felt I was right where the good Lord intended me to be. I was right where He'd planned for me to be many years ago, even before I was formed in my mother's womb. (Remember Jeremiah 1:5?)

I left the event that afternoon and for the first time in my life, I was pelted with a "spiritual hangover" of sorts. I was exhausted and drained, much like those little girls exiting the softball field, but I was still basking in so much joy and peace that the Lord's Word was not going to return void. I was basking in faith that the words I'd spoken to those young ladies earlier that afternoon had made a real impact. I was basking in praise (and shock) that the Lord, in His infinite wisdom, had called a mess-up like me to serve as His vessel.

A few nights later, I was given the opportunity again to share my testimony in a beautiful barn venue adorned with shiplap and gorgeous chandeliers. And as I stood on that stage, the Holy Spirit was undeniably present. Words I had not even rehearsed the night before in my mirror were spilling out of my mouth! God was placing so many new and exciting and fresh ideas on my heart and in my mind, and before I knew it, tears clouded my eyes. And again, He confirmed that I was right where I was meant to be. As I talked about beauty from ashes, He confirmed that every painful thing I've gone through in my life was for that moment. He confirmed it was to encourage and remind others that although this temporary life can be awful crappy at times, He works *all* things for good. He restores joy. He sets captives free. He bestows favor.

First Corinthians 12:27–28 says, "Now you are the body of Christ, and each one of you is a part of it. And God has placed in the church first of all apostles, second prophets, third teachers, then miracles, then gifts of healing, of helping, of guidance, and of different kinds of tongues."

The immeasurable joy of walking in purpose is accessible to everyone in the body of Christ. If you had told me just a few years ago I would be standing in front of people and enthusiastically talking about Jesus Christ, I would have said you were crazy—because although I've been saved a long time, I didn't believe God could use a sinner like me in such a way. I didn't believe I would actually stand in front of a crowd and talk without passing out or peeing my pants.

But the Lord so often calls us to do the things we think we can't do. He equips us. He qualifies us. And He sends us.

Being on fire for God and filled with the Holy Spirit doesn't have to look the same way for you that it looks for me. Maybe God *is* calling you to stand on a stage and publicly declare His love and faithfulness—or maybe He's calling you to do something completely different. Either way, my job isn't more important than yours. Yours isn't more important than mine.

Every position has a divine purpose. Kind of like softball, right?

We are all a vital part in the body of Christ.

A dear friend of mine who works at the local hospital suddenly felt called to spend her lunch breaks visiting with nursing home residents across the street. So every few days, she crosses the busy intersection and pops in to pray with the residents or play a game of Go Fish. She may simply flash someone a smile or ask how they've been or lend an ear and listen to the charming tale of young love in 1947. What she does is beautiful. She shows the love of Christ to the lonely and the lost and the longing, and it's just as important as my preaching to a group of young girls.

As born-again Christians, we all have a calling. And if we aren't the least bit curious about that calling, we need to examine our hearts and our walk with Jesus. We should wake up each day enthusiastically striving to do more and be better than the day before. We should put kingdom work at the top of our priorities—whether we minister to the elderly in a nursing home, anonymously pay someone's electric bill, work in the nursery, volunteer at a soup kitchen, teach Sunday school, dive into missions, or lend an ear. Whatever we do, we should do it devotedly for the Lord, with the ultimate purpose to show the lost that Jesus is the way, the truth, and the life.

If you aren't on fire for God or have yet to find your purpose, tell Him. Look to Him. Tell Him you're ready to roll up your sleeves and get to work. Tell Him you're ready to get on that field. Tell Him to continue to prepare you for your calling and send you when He knows you're ready. Tell Him you're willing. And remember that He doesn't call the qualified; He qualifies the called.

And once He shows you the way and you start walking in your purpose and all that joy and peace just overtakes you, don't get complacent about it. Because we must *never* be satisfied with our walk. We should strive to do more and do better and be called higher and higher each day. If you have breath in your body, you're never done serving and loving and walking in purpose.

I'm a part of the body. You're a part of the body. And, like our physical bodies, each part has a different purpose. But each one is vitally important. And just like those twelve little girls on that softball field, we all have a position to play. We have work to do. We have encouragement and love to give.

CHAPTER 12

Bless This Mess

As I dressed Natalie Ann in her lavender and pink polka-dotted newborn going-home outfit and prepared to leave the hospital, I felt a little panicked. I asked the staff for the instruction manual on how to care for that bald little creature. They laughed. It really irritated me because I hate when people laugh at serious questions.

Those first few months consisted of fear, prayers, and rampant internet searches. I remember talking to our pediatrician's nurse so often I considered making her the sole beneficiary in our will. I remember the sleepless nights and the engorged breasts. I remember the bulk buys of Boudreaux's Butt Paste.

When the newborn phase passed, I had the false sense that things were going to get easier, but boy, was I wrong. Not only was I still buying Butt Paste, but I had to corner an overactive toddler covered in glitter and Goldfish dust to apply it.

And what about the *real fun* stuff: when the three-year-old throws Cheerios at the back of your head while you drive eight hours to Disney World or when your kid throws himself on the floor at Target and you are convinced he will win the 2029 Emmy Award for best lead actor in a dramatic series? When your teen develops an attitude and learns how to roll her eyes and thinks you are the lamest mother in the history of mothers? She won't even let you play air drums in the carpool line anymore without some sassy remark. Those are the times you come unglued.

I'm not proud to admit I went "Hulk" after I told Bennett to get in the bed, but forty-five minutes later he was still putting Transformer stickers on freshly painted walls. I reached the end of my rope when my precious offspring refused to stop screaming about the Lego set I didn't buy him three months ago. I yelled like a banshee when I told eleven-year-old Natalie Ann five times to load the dishwasher but she "forgot because her memory isn't what it used to be." I have experienced overwhelming feelings of frustration and anger that only my precious children can conjure.

I've never verbally or physically hurt my babies, but

I've lost my cool more times than I can count. A dark cloud of guilt hovered over me about that for a long time. I would put them in time-out and then wonder if I was emotionally scarring them for life. I was miserable and felt like an absolute failure. I was certain I was the only mama who blew up when my kindergartener broke a Pier One lamp (it's never the cheap lamp, is it?) and then pathologically lied about it. I was the only mother who blew a gasket at homemade slime embedded in the carpet or permanent marker on my white quilt.

We wish we'd breastfed longer. We wish we'd bought the organic gummies. We wish we'd used our inside voice although our children were using their outside voices and they couldn't hear our inside voice. We wish we'd done so many things differently, and we beat ourselves up over all of it. We have this crazy fear our kids are going to resent us. We fear they aren't going to come home for Christmas when they are older, and if they do, they will bring home a convicted felon named Blade with a pierced septum.

After going to a motherhood class at church, I realized I'm not the only woman who feels this way. I'm not the only yeller in the neighborhood, either. I'm not the only mama who has gone completely ape in a Toys "R" Us aisle. I'm not abusing my daughter when I tell her she can't have Snapchat. I'm not a failure.

However, I am the very mother God intended for my children. He didn't make a mistake when He gave me a forgetful daughter and a strong-willed boy. He didn't make a mistake when He gave me the messiest children on the planet. He knew my weaknesses would come to surface. He knew I would gnaw my nails until they were bloody nubs. He knew I would grit my teeth when Bennett knocked over a huge candy bar display in the grocery store. He knew I would sigh in frustration when Natalie Ann broke another iPad screen. But He also knew I am well equipped to parent them. I have everything they need. I am the perfect mother for them, although I am constantly making mistakes and learning lessons.

When our family went to Florida for Thanksgiving several years ago, I thought it would be a great opportunity to take some beach photos of the kids. I planned to dress them in their matching Christmas outfits and capture a photo that was worthy of Christmas cards and 250 likes on Facebook. Natalie Ann has always been an easygoing child, so she happily complied when I put her in the red corduroy dress with the Christmas tree applique. Bennett, however, wanted no part in donning the matching corduroy Jon Jon. He was determined to wear his Lightning McQueen swim trunks and a two-dollar Garanimals tee, and soon things went sour.

"But, baby," I reasoned with him, "don't you want to look handsome in the picture with Sissy? Don't you want the picture to look nice?"

Newsflash: three-year-olds couldn't care less about a picture looking nice.

He kicked and screamed so much I couldn't even get his fat little legs in the outfit. I just wanted to give up and cry. I wanted to go outside and hotbox a carton of cigarettes. He was going to ruin our Christmas photo. It was the end of the world as I knew it, and I didn't feel fine. (Extra points if you got that R.E.M. reference.)

We didn't take any photos that afternoon. Instead, we went out to eat and I drowned my sorrows in a plate of fried shrimp. When we were leaving the restaurant, I was whining to my family about the boy's noncompliance. I pointed at Bennett, in his swim trunks and dinosaur T-shirt, and grumbled about the missed photo opportunity. An older lady overheard my complaining and approached me.

"You have to pick your battles, dear." She gave me a wink and walked away.

Um, excuse me? Who did this lady think she was? Who was she to tell me to pick my battles? Was she judging me? Did she think I was being a whiny baby just because my whiny baby wouldn't wear a Jon Jon? Did she think letting my kid run all over me was okay? Did she think a Christmas card photo featuring Lightning McQueen was acceptable?

I was fuming over the day's events, but on the ride back to our condo, Stranger Lady's words sank in. I looked over at my precious blond chunk in his car seat watching palm trees out the window. He was happy as a lamb, and I realized he wasn't trying to defy me when he refused to wear what I'd picked out that morning. He just wanted to wear swim trunks on the beach instead of a corduroy romper.

I am proud to say I have learned to pick my battles. As parents, sometimes we have to. I'll never back down when it comes to enforcing rules that keep my children safe or healthy, but Lightning McQueen swim trunks in a beach photo isn't worth me losing my sanity. Ka-chow!

Do your children know they are loved? Do you show them affection? Do you support them? Do you believe in them and thank God for them and pray with them and for them? Yes? Then stop sweating the small stuff. They won't murder you in your sleep because your forehead vein bulged when an eight-ounce glass of grape juice "accidentally" spilled on the new cream couch.

Lord knows my mother made mistakes with me. Maybe letting me watch *Dallas* when I was such a young tot was a bad call, but I didn't grow up and shoot anyone named JR. Maybe pushing me hard to do my best infuriated me when I was a preteen and I hated the world and everyone in it, but I am better for it. I spent every Christmas with her, and I never eloped with a boy with weird piercings. I turned out all right for the most part (except for that time I went to jail, but ignore that) and my children will too.

Motherhood is messy, no doubt, but let us never forget we are blessed.

Blessed in our broke-the-lamp, forgot-to-load-the-dishwasher, lost-their-expensive-coat, rolled-their-eyes, cracked-the-iPad, tracked-mud-through-the-house, lied-about-homework, failed-a-science-test, spilled-the-grape-juice mess.

CHAPTER 13

Eat the Mississippi Mud Cake

Every year, my mother made a Mississippi mud cake for my birthday. The recipe was her mother's and it was unique to our family because she didn't add marshmallows like most Mississippi mud recipes call for. This was because neither my grandmother Lucy nor my mother were fans of the marshmallow. However, they were fans of pecans, so that's what they substituted for cylindrical pieces of sugar, water, and gelatin. I once ordered a slice of Mississippi Mud at a restaurant and they brought out this gooey, white, nut-free mess and I was so offended that I almost asked for the manager.

At every family cookout, Mama made a Mississippi mud cake (sans marshmallows). Oh mercy. Heaven on earth is a slice of warm Mississippi mud cake (sans marshmallows) with a scoop of vanilla ice cream. When Mama died, I framed her handwritten recipe for MMC (sans marshmallows) and set it on my kitchen counter.

What I'm saying is, Mississippi mud cake (sans marshmallows) is life.

It never failed: the day or two after my birthday, I would sit on the couch with the pan in my lap and finish off that delicacy. I didn't care about the calories. Or the carbs. Or the points. Or the bathing suit in the drawer. That cake was joy. Bliss. A 13x9 pan of life's simplest pleasure.

Another simple pleasure in my life is finding a pair of shoes that fit. Bonus points if they don't make me look like a clown at the circus. What does that mean? Well, I'm blessed with oversized feet that make Sasquatches jealous. When I was in school, my mother attempted to comfort me concerning my large feet by saying, "Susannah, supermodels have big feet!"

And I would retort, "So do linebackers, Mama. What's your point?"

Anyway, I cannot accurately put into words how much joy I feel when I walk into a shoe store and walk out with an actual pair of shoes instead of a confirmation number because the salesperson had to order my size from the warehouse. (I want to know where exactly this warehouse is and why don't they open it up to big-footed women like myself. Road trip!)

One night, my sister Carmen, Natalie Ann, Bennett, and I were shoe shopping while on vacation in Florida. My sister has beautiful (small) feet and was trying on shoes that wouldn't even house my big toe. I admired the cute sandals and mumbled and grumbled a little bit about having behemoth feet, but then I heard a sniffle. I looked down and my precious son had tears forming in his eyes. I asked him what was wrong, and he began to cry. "Mama, I just feel so bad you have big feet and can't wear any of these shoes."

"Oh, sweet boy," I said, "don't you cry! They can call the warehouse!"

I love life's simplest pleasures. I love cheering in the stands for my daughter as she storms down the basketball court. I love cuddling with my son on the couch and watching *Teen Titans Go!* I love singing in the car, rocking on the front porch, riding with the windows down on a warm spring day. I love sitting on the beach and reading a good book. I love writing on my back porch while crickets chirp. I love playing on the floor with my dogs. Simple pleasures are the best.

James, the half brother of Jesus, told us in James 1:17 that every good and perfect gift comes "from the Father of the heavenly lights, who does not change like shifting shadows." Mississippi mud cake (sans marshmallows) and cute shoes and pets (I refuse to say fur babies, all right?) are good and perfect gifts. They must come from God!

Those words remind us that our lives, families, talents, abilities, friends, and opportunities—the very things we so often take for granted—are gifts we receive from our heavenly Father's own hand. He showers blessings upon us, not because we have earned them or deserve them, but because He adores us and wants to give abundantly to His children. And God isn't like people who often give gifts with strings attached or expect something from us in return. Instead, He is always faithful, dependable, and unwavering in His consistency. He is the same yesterday, today, and forever.

It seems a simple concept, that all good things come from our heavenly Father, but if we really begin to understand it and relish in it, we will look with awe at beautiful sunrises and starry nights and clouds scattered across the sky. We'll really appreciate the times spent with our loved ones and the warm chocolate cake with a scoop of cold ice cream melting on top. The same good Father who healed our bodies or protected us or gave us children, who blesses us time and time again, painted the sky and aligns the stars for our delight. He gave us our people and invented the cocoa bean. All creation bears witness to His love and majesty.

One of my favorite places in the entire world is Pensacola Beach, Florida. My mother, sister, and I went nearly every summer on a girls' trip. Some of my fondest memories are sitting on the white beach with Mama and Carmen, listening to the waves, talking about life and laughing until we couldn't breathe. And when Natalie Ann was born, I brought her along. I can still see Mama building sandcastles with my precious baby girl wearing a pink seersucker bonnet. Mama took dozens of photos of Natalie Ann with her phone that trip and then asked me how in the world to retrieve the pictures. (She wasn't the most tech savvy, bless her heart. She once called me while I was on a date with Jason and asked me to come home to set her new electric alarm clock because her Big Ben wouldn't wind anymore.)

I adore the smell of the warm, salty air and the sound of waves lapping onto the white sand. I am in awe of the brilliant sunsets that form over the Gulf of Mexico. I don't even mind when seagulls dive into my beach bag and eat my chips. Wait, that's a lie. I don't like that one bit, but I tolerate it.

In all the years I've been to Pensacola Beach, I've never fully credited God with making that serene spot for my pleasure. I've *ooh-ed* and *ahh-ed* at the picturesque ocean, but not until I meditated on James's words did I really appreciate the splendor of Pensacola Beach. Suddenly what was always such a favored place of mine became even more favored. I was in more wonder of the smells and the sights and the sounds. I was more appreciative of the generous helping of tartar sauce and slaw that accompanied my shrimp po-boy at Peg Leg Pete's.

I encourage you to take a moment to recognize that every good gift in your life, including life itself, comes from God's mighty hand. Ask Him to make you more aware and thankful for all He has freely given you. Look at the sunsets, the stars, and even your family, friends, and talents with new appreciation. Praise Him for He is unchanging, and you can rely on His love and mercy every single day.

Life is hectic. Enjoy the simple pleasures. Admire the sunset. Marvel at nature. Buy the shoes if they have your size in stock.

Eat the Mississippi Mud cake.

CHAPTER 14

Praise Him in the Storm

When planning out my future in the pages of my journal in my early twenties, I designed my life with four children. So when Bennett was around two years old, I focused on my third baby. I didn't foresee any problem getting pregnant because it had always been really easy for me. All I needed was a weekend away with Jason and a margarita and *bam*! Set me loose in Target with a baby registry scanner because a little one was on the way.

I didn't care anymore whether I had a girl or a boy. I didn't care that I was so physically sick during both of my pregnancies. I didn't care that I suffered through hormonal acne that left my face looking like Pizza the Hutt

121

from Mel Brooks's classic *Spaceballs*. I didn't care about the bat wings I would grow or the triple chins or the chili-cheese tot cravings at 2:00 a.m. None of that mattered, because the moment both of my children were born, all that discomfort was worth it. Bring on the sleepless nights and the smell of baby vomit hanging in the air. Bring on baby number three.

But my third baby just wouldn't come.

Becoming concerned, I hit the internet message boards on pregnancy and tried to decipher codes like TTC, BD, TWW. (Trying to Conceive, Baby Dance, and Two Week Wait. Why not just type out the words? It literally took three more seconds to just type out the words, people!) We started doing the BD more than I care to think about. Good gracious! It's time to BD again? Didn't we just BD this morning? And this afternoon? And twenty minutes ago?

Do I need to pee on another stick? An ovulation detector stick? A pregnancy test stick? I'm peeing on more sticks than a dog. Do I need to take my temperature? Do I need to eat more raw honey? Jason, are you wearing boxers? Why am I saying "luteal phase" in everyday conversation? With strangers? At Walmart?

I followed the advice of every message board on the internet and nothing happened. I didn't have a baby.

All I had was a pile of urine-soaked sticks in my trash can.

Months turned into years and Jason and I both went

to the doctor. I was poked and prodded in places that should never be poked or prodded. I spent entire days in the clinic wearing nothing but an unflattering paper gown with my feet in stirrups. I took medications, drank herbal teas, and hung upside down for three hours a day. (I didn't really hang upside down, but I would if it meant I would get pregnant.) Every doctor and fertility specialist I saw said I was fine, and I was diagnosed with unexplained infertility.

After my second round of Clomid, a medication that triggers ovulation, I finally stared down at the faint positive sign on the pregnancy test. I was ecstatic to say the least. I eagerly announced the exciting news to my husband and children in the form of a short poem I had written years ago for the very occasion. We rejoiced before I rushed out and bought every pregnancy test at Walgreens. And CVS. I wanted to see those pink lines again. And again. And again.

But each time I took a test, those pink lines became fainter. I went straight to Google for reassurance, which is a terrible idea. I was disheartened because so many women on the message boards posted similar questions about fading lines only to update later that they had miscarried. So, I rushed to see my doctor the following day for blood tests. It was confirmed I was losing the baby. "Spontaneous abortion," they called it.

There was nothing I could do but wait to bleed. I cried on Jason's shoulder at the loss of the child we so desperately wanted. I questioned God. I became angry. I screamed and grumbled and ate a Quarter Pounder and supersized fries to numb the pain. And then I welcomed the finality and the closure as I passed the pregnancy in my home. I sat on my bathroom stool that evening and asked the Lord why this had happened while my mother stood over me with her hands on my shoulders. Thank God, the familiar peace that is only attributed to the Holy Spirit came upon me.

I'd heard "All in God's timing" numerous times while trying to conceive, and I nodded at the words. I believed them to be true, but I never fully surrendered the desires of my heart to the Lord. I thought I'd relinquished control to God, but then I saw a lady on the cover of *The Enquirer*, Betty McBabymaker, seventy-three, had a healthy bundle because she ate guava berries. Yeah, it was in God's timing, but I should probably buy some guava berries. And I found myself putting all of my faith in guava berries instead of God.

"All in God's timing," I'd mumble while I continued to religiously chart my cycle and scribble my calendar with more colors than a bag of Skittles. "All in God's timing," I said while I planned every aspect of pregnancy—down to the very month the baby would be born. I needed a summer baby if I wanted him/her to wear my other children's sleeveless zero-to-three-month onesies in the Rubbermaid totes in the attic. I needed to have this baby before I was thirty-five. I needed more ovulation tests. And thermometers. And raw honey. And guava berries. And herbs. And tea. Plan. Control. Plan. Control. Plan.

And yet, conceiving had nothing to do with my plan.

If I had carried that sweet baby to term, I would have delivered him or her the week before my mother passed away. I could not imagine having a newborn during that time of intense grief and sorrow. I could not imagine bearing the emotional burden of my mother's death while being hormonal and sleep-deprived. My miscarriage was proof that God works all things together for good.

All the things.

The supernatural peace I felt in my bathroom as I miscarried? It was as if God said, "Hey, Susannah, this is in My time. Are you going to give Me *real* control now? Are you going to throw away the pens and the calendars? Are you going to take yourself out of it because it has nothing to do with you? Have you forgotten I'm the Creator of the life you so covet? I will plant the perfect seed within you when I so desire. In My time. My calendar. Not yours."

My miscarriage was necessary for me to realize I'm not the one in control. It was necessary for me to lift my eyes and my hands to Him and say, "Okay, God, I truly surrender and give every desire I have to You."

I've wanted a third baby for six years now, and I've given up control. I've given up the medications and the charts and the message boards. But I haven't given up my faith. I still believe the overwhelming desire to have a third baby has been placed within me by almighty God, and I am continually faithful He will grant my family the desires of our hearts. I am thirty-seven years old, but I have the faith spoken of in Hebrews 11:11: "And by faith even Sarah, who was past childbearing age, was enabled to bear children because she considered him faithful who had made the promise." I don't know if my third child will be formed in my womb or another. I don't know if adoption or foster care is God's plan for our family, but I'm faithful.

Storms come into all of our lives. Sometimes, like radar, we see them ominously approaching. Other times they appear as quickly as the sudden summer shower that causes us to haphazardly throw all our crap in the beach bag and scurry for the hotel. It's important to remember, though, that God doesn't always calm the storm in our lives. Sometimes He calms us in the storm instead. But, no matter what, our best umbrella is faith. And we don't walk around with an umbrella on sunny days, do we? Sometimes a shower is just what we need to exercise our trust in Him.

So I choose to praise Him in the storm.

I also firmly believe life starts at conception, and the child I miscarried wasn't conceived in vain. That child was conceived as a reminder to me, to you, of who is really in control.

One of the most important and simplest lessons we

can learn is to be faithfully content in His will. Not just in terms of family planning, but in all aspects of life. His timing. His plan. His calendar. His will for you is good and perfect.

CHAPTER 15

Sit a Spell

Popsicle juice left sticky streaks on my arms as I sat on the front porch next to my hundred-year-old great-grandmother, Bess Brown. She rocked in a metal-shell-back lawn chair and drank from a Coke can with Kleenex wrapped around it. Her neighbor, Mrs. Mary, would often walk across the green summertime grass to say, "Hello, Ms. Bess!"

And Gran-Gran would respond, "Well, hello there, Mary! Sit a spell."

Mrs. Mary would sit on the swing as Gran-Gran proceeded to spin hour-long yarns about her childhood. If Mrs. Mary had somewhere to be those afternoons, she was late.

Maybe I'll be blessed enough to live to a hundred and sit on a metal lawn chair entertaining my neighbors with stories of my youth. Maybe I'll drink out of Dr. Pepper cans with Kleenex wrapped around the bottom while my great-grandchildren lick melted sugar from their hands. Maybe I'll one day say, "Sit a spell," and I'll tell these tales.

∿

In the summer of 1990 I was nine years old. Mama and I were headed to Texas in Mama's big Oldsmobile with her Sunday school teacher and dear friend, Mrs. Murphy, and Mrs. Murphy's granddaughter, Jessica. We were taking Jessica back to her home state after she'd spent the summer with Mrs. Murphy here in Tennessee.

Jessica was a few years older than me, and I thought of her as a big sister. Mrs. Murphy was older than Mama, and Mama thought of her as a big mama. She'd been my mother's rock since Grandmother Lucy had passed away a few years before. What a blessing she was not only to Mama, but to our entire family. She was with me when that casual EMT told me my father was dead.

My mother, being the humorous lady she was, always had Mrs. Murphy in stitches. Mama thrived on making Mrs. Murphy laugh so hard that her entire body jiggled like Jell-O. I can see her now, laughing and bouncing as little beads of sweat broke out on her hairline of pretty auburn curls. Mrs. Murphy's laugh—oh my mercy—it was loud and boisterous and contagious. When she was really tickled, she'd snort. Hearing that precious lady chortle and guffaw made my heart nine kinds of happy.

So the lively, laughing, snorting bunch that we were traveled across Arkansas to get to the Lone Star State, and we decided to spend our first night in Hot Springs. Although we only lived a few hours from both the Ozarks and the Appalachian ranges, it was my first time to visit the mountains. My mother had spent a lot of her childhood camping and being surrounded by nature, and she'd had her fill of it. She'd had enough dirt and dust and bugs and fishing to last a lifetime, so she wasn't keen on vacationing among such things. Instead, she always opted to take us to the beach, and we drove down to Florida every summer of my youth. My mother was happiest on the sand and listening to the waves. She had no need for that camping stuff. She said we had enough pine trees in our own backyard.

But, as the big Oldsmobile navigated up the dark and winding road to our cabin and my ears began to pop while we ascended higher and higher, I was ecstatic. This was new and uncharted terrain for me.

When we finally arrived at our cozy cabin in the Ozarks, my mama began spouting off rules about staying away from cliffs and being wary of bears and ticks with Lyme disease. Mrs. Murphy, howling with laughter at Mama's paranoia, patted me on the back to assure me that everything was going to be fine.

We had a lovely evening in that cabin talking and playing board games we found in the hall closet. Mama always brought a picnic basket of snacks for our road trips, so I scarfed down a nutritionally balanced meal of Little Debbie snacks and multiple cans of Dr. Pepper. I ran through the cabin like a sugar fiend, annoying everyone.

When it was time to turn in, Mrs. Murphy was forced to sleep alone at the opposite side of the cabin. We'd been on enough road trips with her to know that her snoring could wake the dead. Sleep was impossible in her presence. She understood, and we banished her to her sleeping quarters and told her to shut the door.

Mama and I piled into one bed, and Jessica slept in the bed next to ours. We spent a long time listening to the crickets chirping and bullfrogs croaking outside the cabin. Even Mama, the beach bum, commented on what a peaceful sound it was. We told stories and laughed and had an unusually lengthy conversation about Jessica's crush on Scott Baio.

Only moments before we all drifted off to sleep, our hearts full of the day's laughter, jokes, and joy, a loud noise jilted us all awake. It wasn't Mrs. Murphy's snoring, no; but it was a startling and somewhat disturbing sound just the same. It sounded like something was rummaging through the garbage outside. Then we heard a loud bang of the garbage can's tin lid hitting the gravel.

Because I'd recently seen *Harry and the Hendersons*, my heart began to pound in my throat as I envisioned a

Sasquatch trying to break into the cabin. Was this how it was going to end? My nine years were going to come to a halt in the clutches of a bloodthirsty Bigfoot that wasn't nearly as nice as Harry?

I clung to my mother's arm while she sat up in the bed and listened carefully. She whispered for Jessica and me to stay there, and she slowly crept over to the window.

"What is it, Mama?" I screeched through trembling lips.

"I see something moving out there," she said.

Well, that didn't ease my fears at all. In my best Vinton Harper (remember *Mama's Family?*) voice, I mustered a, "Thanks a lot, Mama!" as Jessica snickered beneath her covers.

"I'll go see what it is." She headed toward the bedroom door. I sprung from the bed and clung to her hip, begging her not to leave me. Jessica joined us, and although she wasn't quite as nervous as I was, it was evident she didn't want to be left alone either.

The three of us, holding tightly to one another, shuffled through the dark cabin to the soundtrack of Mrs. Murphy's thunderous booming in her bedroom. We reached the door and Mama flipped on the porch light and looked out the window. With my head buried in the back of Mama's nightgown and Jessica's head buried into the back of mine, Jessica said, "Mrs. Susan, what is it?"

"Oh! Sweet Lord!" Mama exclaimed.

"It's a Sasquatch, isn't it?" I tightly shut my eyes and waited for the beast to knock down the door and devour me as a midnight snack. I just knew I would taste like a Little Debbie Fudge Round.

"It's worse," Mama howled.

I peered around Mama's nightgown and looked out the window to see a monstrous furry creature sitting on its hind legs on the picnic table. We eyed it for only a second, nothing between us and rabies but a thin plate of glass, as it used its humanlike hands to shove garbage into its mouth. And then it looked right at us, made some kind of aggressive chattering noise, and *lurched* toward the window.

We all let out bloodcurdling screams and sprinted back to our beds. Mama and I both hid under the blankets and latched on to each other.

"Sweet Jesus! It's a ghastly oversized rat!" Mama panted. It was a known fact that my mother abhorred rodents and cats and birds. You don't find many rodents or cats or birds at the beach—except for seagulls. But she'd take a seagull over a raccoon any day!

Once we'd calmed down and the sounds of the raccoon chattering and rustling through the garbage finally ceased, we began to laugh again. We laughed at my mother's unnatural raccoon fear. We laughed because I had been certain it was Bigfoot. We laughed because Mrs. Murphy snored her way through the entire ordeal. We laughed because I thought Scott Baio had a funny last name. My fear subsided, and that giant dose of laughter certainly helped.

The next morning, as I cleaned the mess that the raccoon had left behind, Little Debbie wrappers and Dr. Pepper cans strewn all over the campsite, I heard Mrs. Murphy snickering and snorting uncontrollably inside.

"A rac—*snort*—coon, Susan! You were terrified of a rac—*snort*—coon!" she exclaimed as tears rolled down her face and left streaks in her plum blush.

"Rabies is nothing to play around with, Mrs. Murphy!" Mama exclaimed.

That raccoon wasn't much of a threat, but it certainly terrified that overweight nine-year-old girl clinging to her mother's nightgown. And even today, when I'm scared or anxious or downright afraid, I think back to that night in Arkansas so many years ago. I think back on the roaring laughter that made it all worthwhile.

Sweet, sweet laughter makes so many things worthwhile.

〰

During my tenth summer, Mama agreed to care for her friend's elderly mother while her regular caregiver was out of town. Her tasks would include giving Mrs. Brooks her medication, fixing her meals, and sleeping in her beautiful, antique-adorned guest bedroom in case Mrs. Brooks needed anything during the night.

Everyone in our small town knew Mrs. Brooks. She

was a wealthy widow who lived in a big, beautiful home on a corner lot in the historic district. She was in her late eighties but was still a stunning woman. Her gorgeous silver hair was long and thick and always pinned into a neat bun. She wore a lot of jewelry and fuchsia blush and matching lipstick, and even though most of that lipstick ended up on her teeth, she still had a lovely smile. Mrs. Brooks was definitely the classiest and most stylish octogenarian I knew! (Granted, I didn't know *that* many octogenarians.)

Mrs. Brooks was also half deaf. She asked everyone to repeat themselves a minimum of five times, although people yelled at her loudly enough for residents in the neighboring county to hear.

So, on the day my mother was to sit with Mrs. Brooks, we pulled into the driveway shaded with massive magnolia trees and climbed up the wide, painted porch steps. Mother rang the doorbell. And she rang it again.

And she rang it for nearly ten minutes.

I stood on the old wraparound porch while my mother peered through the tall windows and called Mrs. Brooks's name. Bored, I swatted at flies and complained about the sweltering heat and the heavy humidity as sweat streamed down my back.

Finally, Mrs. Brooks heard the doorbell. Through the window on the front door, we saw her petite, frail body slowly making its way to let us in. I couldn't wait for the cool, refreshing air inside her home to welcome me.

But when the precious little lady opened the door, my mother and I were pelted with a draft of thick, hot air. It wasn't cooler inside the house. In fact, it felt about twenty degrees warmer.

She showed us to the bedroom where we would be sleeping. Two of the three windows were open, allowing the stagnant, sweltering air to suffocate the room.

"Mrs. Brooks, do you want me to close those windows and turn on the window unit?" Mama asked, beads of perspiration covering her forehead.

"What?" Mrs. Brooks asked.

And my mother repeated (*read: screamed*) the question five more times before Mrs. Brooks answered, "No, dear. Running the air costs too much."

I couldn't believe my warm, red ears. Mrs. Brooks was the wealthiest lady in town! How could she think crisp, cool air conditioning was too much of a splurge?

"It's loud too," she said as my mother and I exchanged a glance of confusion. It was hard to believe this woman could hear the AC unit when she couldn't hear my mother yelling right in her face.

So we went about our day. We helped Mrs. Brooks chop vegetables in the kitchen and listened to tales about her family, all while Mama and I dripped with sweat. Mama fixed her a glass of cold iced tea and sat with her on the front porch to watch cars sail down the sleepy street. I sat on the front steps, drenched to the bone and wishing I was in my cool house across town.

The sun went down, but the temperature did not. My mother helped Mrs. Brooks to bed and came into our bedroom, her blonde hair frizzing from the dense humidity.

"I can't deal with this heat, Susannah! I'm going to die!"

I agreed as I dressed in cotton pajamas and Mama put on her nightgown and we both wiped the sweat from our faces. Our sticky backs touched each other as we lay in the small wrought-iron bed while crickets chirped outside the opened windows.

Mama sat up every few minutes to fan herself and get a drink of water from the bedside table. She shook the collar of her damp nightgown to create air flow, and she huffed and puffed before putting her head back on the pillow.

Finally, Mama couldn't take it anymore. She got up and shut the windows and turned on the window unit. When it roared to life, I hopped out of the bed and Mama and I stood in front of the air conditioner. We smiled and basked in the chill. Sweet relief! It was heaven!

Suddenly we heard Mrs. Brooks call from her bedroom at the back of the house, "Girls! That air conditioner isn't on, is it?"

As if we were two children in trouble, my mother quickly switched it off and threw the windows back open. We jumped into the sticky bed, our hearts pounding, and we lay there in the dark, without so much as a breeze blowing through the opened windows.

Hot. Stagnant. Suffocating. Torture.

And then my mama started laughing. She laughed so hard that she had to sit up in the bed to catch her breath. Like a little kid, my mother couldn't stop cackling.

"Mama, what's wrong with you?"

"How did she possibly hear the air conditioner? She couldn't hear a train hitting a power plant!"

And then I started laughing too. And before long, we were both guffawing at our situation—being stuck in the broiling home of a wealthy widow who wouldn't splurge on air conditioning. We laughed, without fear of Mrs. Brooks hearing us, and we worked up even more of a sweat. Tears of laughter streamed down my mother's face and mixed with the perspiration. The louder we laughed, the louder the crickets chirped.

We didn't sleep a wink that hot summer night.

But we sweated.

And we laughed.

When I was a chubby little checker, we lived in a beautiful country house surrounded by ten acres of rolling land. Cattle grazed in the fields and defecated by the picturesque pond. It was truly a gorgeous place to live, and I was blessed to have spent several years, ages six through ten, calling that my home.

I really loved the dozens of hiding places on that property, my favorite being the huge satellite dish nestled in the corner of the yard. Do you know what a man hated to hear back in 1989? "Honey, there's static on the Quasar. Will you go outside and adjust the satellite before *Knot's Landing* comes on?"

Anyway, one day I crawled into the bowl of the gigantic dish that resembled something produced by NASA, and I saw my white mutt, Buttermilk, walking along the fence at the back of the property, about a hundred yards away. Yes, the dog's name was Buttermilk. He was a creamy white kind of color. You know? Like buttermilk.

"Buttermilk!" I called to him from the dish, eager to play with him and pick the cockleburs and fat, blood-filled ticks that resembled kidney beans from his ears.

"Buttermilk, come here!"

And then Buttermilk suddenly appeared, from the opposite side of the house. The white creature walking along the barbed-wire fence wasn't my mutt.

I watched the animal closely, and I realized that it wasn't a dog at all. It was a huge animal with a long white tail dragging the ground. In fact, it looked like a cat. It was a ginormous cat with the longest and weirdest tail I'd ever seen.

"Hey," I yelled to the creature. "Hey, cat!"

And the cat looked at me.

And it screamed like a woman.

Stunned, I ran as fast as my short little legs would take me, making sure that Buttermilk and his cockleburs and ticks were following me.

"Mama!" I screamed.

I called for my mother, and I found her watching the critically acclaimed makeup-tip video by Donna Mills, *The Eyes Have It*, on the VCR in her bedroom. Mama's eyes were covered in blue eyeliner as she studied the television screen.

"What?" Mama asked, checking herself in the bedroom mirror and applying a dollop of pink eyeshadow.

"Some kind of animal screamed at me. It screamed, Mama! *It screamed like a woman!*"

Mother shot over to her bedroom window and looked to the backyard. She saw the animal, now only thirty or forty yards away, and she gasped.

"Sweet Jesus, Susannah! That's some kind of panther!"

Panthers aren't native to West Tennessee, all right?

Mama sprinted to the huge cordless phone, pulled up the three-foot-long antennae, and dialed animal control. We personally knew the animal-control guy, Catfish (yes, Skeeter's stepson). He'd been to our house on several occasions to remove opossums from the crawl space and woodchucks from the front porch.

When Catfish showed up, the animal was gone. As Mama and I frantically described what we'd seen, he let out a hearty laugh of disbelief.

My daddy came home a while later. As Mama and I frantically described what we'd seen, he let out a hearty laugh too.

My mother called twenty-three friends that afternoon.

As she frantically described what we'd seen, they all let out hearty laughs.

I called one friend that afternoon. She wasn't home.

Weeks later, a news report surfaced about a fellow in a neighboring town who was arrested for keeping exotic animals caged on his farm. An emu went missing. And some kind of weird lizard. And a panther. An albino panther.

They never found that albino panther.

And nobody let out a hearty laugh.

∿

During my seventeenth summer, I worked at Ward's Dry Cleaners in my hometown. It was the worst job ever. They didn't even allow me a calculator to figure out the tax. Who did I look like? Good Will Hunting?

One afternoon, a guy walked in and casually said, "Hi, I dropped off some pants this morning. I left some marijuana in the pocket."

Stunned and looking for candid cameras, I muttered, "Um, what?"

"I left a small bag of marijuana in my pants pocket. Would you get it for me?" He smiled.

"Do you just want the pants back?" I asked, confusion covering my face.

"No, just the bag of weed will be fine. Here is my ticket." He handed the receipt to me.

I hesitantly nodded and walked to the back of the building, the temperature at 345 degrees, and began rummaging through a pile of dirty laundry. I found the pants with instructions to be laundered and heavily starched, and sure enough there was a small bag of dope in the pocket. Looking around for witnesses, I retrieved the drugs and quickly walked back to the front of the store.

The pothead was gone, but standing in his place was a local police officer. I let out a sound that resembled lungs collapsing, and I threw my back against the wall, gripping the bag of marijuana in my hand as the cop and the older lady I worked with looked at me.

"Everything okay, Susannah?" Dry Cleaner Lady asked.

"Sh-sh-sure." I gulped, contraband hidden in my innocent seventeen-year-old hands.

"That young man said he would be back later," she replied as she tagged the police officer's uniform. "Said he left something in his pocket? Did you find it?"

"Uh, yes, ma'am. I got it," I mumbled as perspiration dripped from my forehead.

"What was it?" Dry Cleaner Lady asked as I locked eyes with the police officer and tightly squeezed the Ziploc bag of drugs.

"Uh . . ." My eyes darted around the room while I tried to conjure up a lie. "Paper. It's just a note or something. I've got it."

"You can put it back in the office in the lost-and-found

pile," she said, quickly figuring the math for the officer's items.

I was expected to put a bag of weed in the lost-and-found pile?

My boss was in the office reading a newspaper. I shoved the drugs deep into my pocket without him noticing, and I scribbled some lines on a sheet of paper, folded it, and threw it in the small lost-and-found pile of sunglasses and keychains.

Hours later, Pusherman returned.

"Did you find it?" he asked, calm, cool, casual.

"You've no idea what I've been through! I don't appreciate it!" I exclaimed as I reached into my pocket and threw the stash of marijuana at him.

He nodded, tucked his drugs in his pocket, and walked out the front door.

I can look back and laugh on it now, but for three hours, at the age of seventeen, I was laundering more than laundry.

I was a dry cleaner drug dealer.

ᴧ

And right about now, my hundred-year-old body will finally get up from my metal lawn chair, walk inside, curl up in a cozy recliner, and take a nap.

Thanks for sitting a spell.

CHAPTER 16

Cancel Your Guilt Trip

I swiped a grape from my hometown grocery store's produce department when I was about eight or nine. Before the dirty purple sphere made it down my throat, I knew I was destined to burn in hell for stealing. The guilt was so unbearable I would never again go grocery shopping with my mother without remembering my sin. That was the first and last time I ate fruit that couldn't be validated with a receipt.

I've always had a guilty spirit. I felt guilty for big things like lying to my mother about my whereabouts and coming home after curfew. And little things like shoving stuff under my bed instead of putting it in its proper place.

Guilt followed me right into adulthood like a rabid monkey on my back. Every hangover consisted of excessive dry mouth, nausea, and a heaping side of guilt. On the way home from a shopping trip, I would look over at the clutch in my passenger seat that cost more than a ruby-studded suitcase and be overwhelmed with guilt. I felt guilty for bashing my husband in the head with the stainless-steel trashcan when he forgot to take out the garbage. I felt guilty for making Natalie Ann eat cafeteria gopher intestines with her choice of brown or white gravy instead of making her lunch. I felt guilty for making Bennett give up his favorite stuffed animal as punishment for being a Grade-A turd. I felt guilty for feeding my children junk food that contained more chemicals than an aerosol can of body spray. I was no better than Joan Crawford with a closet full of wire hangers.

I shouldn't have talked about her. I shouldn't have talked about him. I shouldn't have gone. I shouldn't have spoken. I shouldn't have written that. I shouldn't have laughed at that. I shouldn't have committed to that. I shouldn't have said that. I shouldn't have thought that. I shouldn't have done that. I shouldn't. I shouldn't. I shouldn't.

I should have been nice. I should have smiled. I should have called. I should have gone. I should have spoken. I should have written that. I should have read that. I should have committed to that. I should have said that. I should have thought that. I should have done that. I should. I should. I should.

My biggest regret is the last conversation I had with my mother. The day before she died, we had a petty argument over the phone. I stood at my bathroom counter with the phone tightly squeezed between my palm, my forehead vein bulging, and I screamed at my mama. I screamed horrible things to her, and the last words I said before I slammed the phone down to my vanity were, "I'm done with you, Mama! I am done!"

My blood pressure at an all-time high, I continued to rant aloud to my image in the bathroom mirror as I applied eyeshadow and prepared to see Hall and Oates with Jason for our tenth wedding anniversary. I ranted and I raved and I tried to validate the malicious words I'd spoken just minutes before to my mother.

Mama and I—our bond, our relationship was so resilient, so beautiful, but so messy at times. We were identical—both bullheaded and stubborn. That's why we argued that day. She didn't agree with me, and she was too proud to admit her wrongs. I was too proud to admit mine. I was too proud to bite my tongue.

But we would make up tomorrow. We always did. And, of course, I wasn't really "done" with my mother. She was my mother! She was my best friend. She was my spiritual mentor. She was my everything. My mother was everything to me.

As Jason and I ate dinner for our anniversary that night, I was still fuming over the argument that afternoon with Mama. Then I remembered the Bible verse I had received via text that very morning. Proverbs 15:1: "A gentle answer turns away wrath, but a harsh word stirs up anger." As I cut my steak before the concert, I told Jason, "I should have followed the advice of Proverbs today. I should have kept calm with Mama. I shouldn't have said that. I shouldn't have been so stubborn."

I shouldn't. I shouldn't. I shouldn't.

I had every intention to make it right the next day. I had every intention to let things cool off and call Mama and apologize and forget it ever happened. We would tell each other how much we loved the other and talk about the concert and my kids and what kind of cream I should put on a weird rash on Bennett's leg. I would make it right.

But my mother died the next day.

And the last words I spoke to her were, "I'm done with you, Mama."

God, it still breaks my heart.

When I found out my mother was dead, the first cohesive sentence I put together was, "I told Mama I was done with her! I broke her heart! That's what killed her, Jason! I broke her heart." And I believed that for months after Mama passed away. My mother, who had raised me on her own for so many years and provided every need and prayed over me and for me and loved me unconditionally, surely died because I'd been so vicious to her. My words had worried her and distressed her to the point of cardiac arrest. Her baby girl, her everything, told her she didn't want to have anything more to do with her. How that must have grieved her spirit.

That guilt trumps swiping a grocery store grape any day.

As the months passed, the shock of her death wore off, the deep sorrow was lessened, the mourning waned more than it waxed. But the regret remained. It ate me alive—that disgusting, painful, gnawing, cancerous regret. Thinking about it for only half a second took me to an abysmal, dark, dreaded place in my soul that was too painful to acknowledge. I got on my knees and begged God for forgiveness of that sin and my words more times than I can count. I often stood on my back patio and whispered up to the heavens on a clear night, "I'm so sorry, Mama. Please forgive me."

My grief counselor told me I had to let it go. She told me Mama would have forgiven me had she lived long enough to get the chance. In fact, she probably forgave me as soon as I said it. Didn't I immediately forgive my toddler when he told me I was the meanest mommy in the world because I didn't let him ride his scooter in oncoming traffic? My grief counselor reminded me Mama isn't in heaven worrying about the last words I spoke to her. She is spending her eternity in a place so real and pure and gorgeous, praising our Savior, and isn't concerned with the matters of this earth. She feels no sorrow at my actions and words. She isn't angry with me.

And I knew that. I really did know that, but like the good memories I clung to, the bad memories were still there. They attempted to gnaw and bite and rip away at my soul. Those spiteful words were always there, even as I cheered at my children's ball games or made funny videos on Facebook. The regret was there.

Finally, utterly overwhelmed by the regret, the guilt, the blame, I truly surrendered it to God. I threw my hands in the air and declared I couldn't live with that dark cloud hovering over me all the time. And He spoke to me, gently, *I've already forgiven you of this. Why do you keep bringing it up?*

"But, God . . ."

I've already forgiven you of this. Why do you keep bringing it up?

"But, God, please just tell Mama . . ."

This is already forgiven. Why do you keep bringing it up?

Conviction and condemnation aren't the same thing. Conviction is a gentle nudge from the Holy Spirit that corrects us when we've done wrong. Conviction puts us back on the right path and encourages lessons to be learned. It leads to repentance. Conviction led me to ask both God and my mother for forgiveness of my harsh words. Condemnation, however, is not from the Holy Spirit. It is a constant reminder of our wrongs. We often cling to condemnation because we feel we deserve it. If we feel bad enough about something all the time, it will lessen what we did, right? It's agonizing and relentless guilt on steroids, and I ain't talkin' Prednisone. I'm talking that stuff that makes testicles shrink down to the size of marbles.

We can't live in peace when we are consumed by condemnation. I certainly can't. I can't be a good wife or mother or friend or Christian or person if I'm swallowed up in remorse and daily, hourly, minutely reminders of my countless mistakes.

Jesus hung on that old, rugged cross to save the world, not condemn it. He hung there, bloodied and beaten, for every sin I've committed. For every sin I will commit. For every harsh word I've spoken. For every wrong thing I've done. For every grape I've stolen.

I did what I did and it wasn't right. I'm not a perfect wife or mother or friend or Christian or person 100 percent of the time. No one is. Maybe I'm the biggest disaster to walk on two legs—covered in stubble because I should have shaved and now I feel guilty that my husband gashed his hand open on my sharp knee. Three stitches, dear? Oh, bother. It's all my fault.

But I'm letting go of the guilt. Jesus forgives me, so I'm forgiving myself.

This doesn't mean that I'm going to start doing what I darn well please without worrying about the outcome or consequences. I'm not completely ridding myself of a guilty conscience. That guilty conscience is probably the only thing that has kept me from burning down the Chuck E. Cheese's. (I shouldn't have said that. If it actually burns down, I will be the first suspect.) But I have made the decision to quit being my own worst enemy.

We will make mistakes. It's inevitable, and we can't second-guess every word we speak or every decision we make, whether it regards our spouses, children, parents, finances, or hobbies. We can't continue to go through life feeling like the bad guy. We can't continue to hang our heads in shame and label ourselves as "World's Worst _____."

I can't. You can't.

(Unless you're an ax murderer or something. Then you should feel incredibly guilty and turn yourself in to local authorities.)

But if you yelled at your kid for setting fire to the couch or you cheated on your diet with a bulk-sized vat of Nutella, then, well, don't beat yourself up about it. If you've hurt the ones closest to you, repent of it and move on. If you've done something you don't think can be washed away by the blood of Jesus, think again.

CHAPTER 17

Comfort Others and You Will Be Comforted

Grief is a tricky thing. It is deep and substantial. It is a void—an emptiness that is literally capable of taking your breath away. And when my mother died, I felt the need to share mine. I started with selfish motives. I was all riled up and had pent-up grief inside that had to be let out. So I shared it for my own good. For my own healing. But as I continued to write, the feedback I received changed everything.

I soon learned grief is a universal language. Everyone has lost someone they've loved. They've longed for the way things were, for their mother's laugh, their grand-father's stories. They've wished things could go back to the way they were a year, five years, ten years, thirty years ago. Death leaves a scar on hearts. Like all scars, they get easier to accept, but they remain.

As I read comments on my blog posts, my pain was no longer mine. Theirs was no longer theirs. It was ours. And I knew I was called to point people to the great Comforter.

Then on September 20, 2016, I drove to the shady country cemetery where both my parents are buried. September 20 is my father's birthday, and it is also the day my mother was reunited with him in heaven. What a celebration that must've been. I'm sure it was much better than a trip to Red Lobster.

I sat in my car with two bouquets of flowers, and on a whim, I reached for my phone. I looked like I'd been through three wars and a goat roping. My face was swollen and red, and my eyes were bloodshot. I think I had a snot stain on my nose, but I followed the tugging on my heart and sat my phone on my dashboard as I had hundreds of times when making a funny video. I pressed record and just started rambling. I rambled and I cried and I reached for my Bible in the passenger seat desperate for answers. Desperate for comfort.

I had to stop the video to wipe my nose and collect myself. But, through the Holy Spirit, I received the strength I needed, and I pressed record again. Thankfully,

I didn't ramble quite as much the second video attempt. I got right to the point of why I was there—to place flowers on both my parents' graves. And I addressed the questions I'd asked myself, asked God, for so many years.

Why did Mama have to die after I'd spoken such cruel words to her?

Why did Daddy have to die while I was home alone with him?

Why was I a thirty-four-year-old orphan?

Why couldn't I get pregnant?

Why did I miscarry?

Why, God, why the loss and the pain?

And the Lord gave me the answer in 2 Corinthians 1:3–7, which I read aloud on the video:

Praise be to the God and Father of our Lord Jesus Christ, the Father of compassion and the God of all comfort, who comforts us in all our troubles, so that we can comfort those in any trouble with the comfort we ourselves receive from God. For just as we share abundantly in the sufferings of Christ, so also our comfort abounds through Christ. If we are distressed, it is for your comfort and salvation; if we are comforted, it is for your comfort, which produces in you patient endurance of the same sufferings we suffer. And our hope for you is firm, because we know that just as you share in our sufferings, so also you share in our comfort.

I posted the video and waited for the comments to roll in. I was nervous because I didn't know how it would be received. I imagined comments like, "Who is this nut job crying in a cemetery?"

"Take a chill pill, lady!"

"Bless her heart. She needs some help."

"Someone give her a wet wipe to remove that dollop of snot from her face!"

But instead, amazing things began to happen. My inbox was flooded with messages from people I'll never meet this side of heaven—people who were suffering substantially and asking, "Why?" Good golly, that was a powerful moment in my life.

One comment that really stuck out to me was from a young woman who had contemplated suicide only moments before seeing the video. But, when she looked at all her life's hardships in a new way, in the comforting way Paul described trials in 2 Corinthians, her burdens were lifted. She said she really felt the Lord come to her at that moment and let her see the point of it all. She finally had purpose in her pain. She knew she was being instructed not to take her own life, but to help someone else find theirs.

That video of me snotty-crying in a cemetery wasn't for me. It wasn't to say, "Hey, look at everything I've been through! Give me some pity, people! Help me feel better about it all!" That video was for God's glory.

Reading those verses from 2 Corinthians became my

lightbulb moment. That became my heartbeat, my life's song. That became the basis for this entire book. That gave me clarity. That gave me answers. So, what's the reason for the pain? For the loss? So I could, in turn, receive God's comfort and comfort others.

ᴧ

After my daddy died, I leaned on the shoulders of Mr. Charles, my mama's first husband. I've grown to admire Charles more and more over the years. He taught me that family isn't defined by blood. He taught me that doing the right thing isn't always easy.

In 1960, hundreds of students had gathered in the school auditorium to watch a play about Davy Crockett. The young actor playing the part of Crockett was a female—a voluptuous, well-endowed eighth grader. She bounced across the stage in a coonskin cap, and when she declared, "You will find me standing up to my *rack*, as the people's faithful representative," three students in the audience laughed uncontrollably and were sent to the principal's office.

One of those students was my thirteen-year-old mother. She had no idea the two boys with her in the office would one day be her husbands.

Mama officially met one of those boys later in high school. Being from a small town, their parents knew one another, but they had never been friends. Charles was tall, handsome, and blond-headed, and he soon became Mama's first steady boyfriend. Like my mother, he was incredibly fun and witty, and they went together like peas and carrots. He was the one who drove her home after school most days as they passed Betsy pretending to park her mother's Chevrolet on the street.

Right out of high school, Charles went to work for the telephone company in town and my mother went to beauty school. Soon after, they married in an elegant wedding at First Methodist Church downtown Brownsville and situated in their first home, a small brick house near the railroad tracks.

My brother, Keith, was born first—a bouncy little baby boy with a head full of thick, dark hair and his parents' quick wit. And three years later, my beautiful and kind-hearted sister, Carmen, came along with poker-straight blonde hair that I resent to this day. (Humidity is not her enemy as it is mine. One drop of water in the air and I look like I have fur.) Charles was with Mama when her father, Hilliard, finally lost his long battle with emphysema. He was with Mama when she received the phone call that her baby sister, Linda, had been killed by a drunk driver. They went through so much together and loved each other fiercely. They remained married for over a decade.

My father, Billy Brown, worked with Mr. Charles at the telephone company. All the soap-opera-esque details were withheld from me by my mother, but she left Charles for my father in 1979.

You guessed it. That other kid in the office for laughing at Davy Crockett's rack was my daddy.

Mr. Charles had every reason in the world to be resentful and angry and bitter with both my mother and father. His wife left him for his friend and co-worker. That's Jerry Springer–type stuff. And yet he somehow forgave them both, and my mother and Charles successfully coparented my siblings. I was used to Mr. Charles being around to pick up Carmen or Keith from our house or even stopping to talk to Daddy while he mowed our yard. He still visited his ex-mother-in-law, my grandmother Lucy, for a slice of her pecan pie or to drop off a batch of tomatoes. He was part of our family.

When my daddy died that cold November day, Mr. Charles was one of the first to arrive at my house. I will never forget standing in my driveway with sock feet on the frigid pavement and Mr. Charles pulling me close to him. I buried my head into his dark coat while he rubbed my back.

It was understood right then, I think, between the both of us, that he was going to step up to be my father figure. Although his high school sweetheart had left him for my father and I was conceived out of that matrimony, he was going to love me anyway.

And that's exactly what he did.

After Daddy died, Mr. Charles came to every holiday meal my mother cooked and always brought the

Honeybaked ham. He scooped the disgusting dead chicken from the Thanksgiving table that fateful day; he kept my dog, Peaches, when we went on vacation; and he let me borrow his truck to ride around town when I was fifteen.

We watched baseball together in his living room and ate pizza. Jason, Keith, my brother-in-law, Doug, and Mr. Charles stood around the grill on our patio and told jokes that sometimes had me covering my toddler's ears. Mr. Charles kept us all laughing constantly, and one of my favorite things in life was being wrapped in his arms and engulfed in the scent of his cologne. He always smelled so good. He showered me with gifts and we talked on the phone for hours each week. On my wedding day, he walked me down the aisle. And when both my children were born, he stood outside the hospital room and waited to meet his grandchildren.

He was the man in my life that he did not have to be.

When he didn't show up for Grandparents' Day lunch at my daughter's elementary school in September 2011, I knew something was wrong. My mother, brother, and sister couldn't reach him on the phone at his house he'd shared with my mother when they were married. And a few hours later, it was confirmed by Mr. Charles's brother that he'd had a heart attack and died in the home.

For nineteen years, Mr. Charles filled the void my father's death had left in 1992. When he was gone, I really felt for the first time that I didn't have a dad. I was utterly heartbroken at the loss. His death was the reason I started my blog, *Write, Rinse, Repeat.* The first post I ever published online was called "My Two Dads." (Yes, I stole the title from the eighties sitcom.)

I like to think, though, when Mr. Charles was reunited in glory with his family and friends, that he saw my father. I like to think Daddy greeted him with a smile and a firm handshake.

"I know what you've done. Thank you," Daddy said.

"She still misses you," answered Mr. Charles.

I like to think Mr. Charles shared stories with my father as they walked along a street of gold. Stories of how I had matured and married and had beautiful children of my own. How my daughter plays piano effortlessly and my son always has a toy truck in his hand. I like to think Daddy thanked Charles again for being there when he couldn't. And for being there for my mother, being her friend and confidant, when he couldn't.

Charles was my mother's first love, and she certainly mourned his death. They were always talking on the phone about the grandchildren or venting to the other about politics. They often sat around remembering stories from high school and leaving us all in stitches. She said to me not long before she died, "I miss Charles so much. I can't wait to get to heaven to see him again."

Now that Mama, Daddy, and Mr. Charles have all passed away, I do feel as if I've lost three parents. Each one played a different yet equally important part in my life. Two of them gave me life, but all three of them gave me unconditional love.

After Dad died, Mr. Charles often shared stories about him with me because he knew it would bring me joy, and he never had an ounce of resentment in his voice. I'm sure there were times he looked at me as a reminder of my mother's leaving him for another man, and yet he treated me like I was his own.

I'm well aware that we are instructed to forgive others as Christ forgives us, but I will admit that's not one of my favorite parts of the Bible. I can get on board with "do not murder" and "do not steal," but I've always had a hard time letting it go when someone has done me wrong. I'm still kind of angry with the boy who showed up on my doorstep with another girl's mark on his neck. When I see a particular classmate, who stole my Lisa Frank notebook in sixth grade and lied about it, I smile at her but still wish I'd pressed charges and she'd spent a few years on the inside. I've forgiven the girls who bullied me in middle school, but I have no interest in being in their presence. And I think if Jason were to leave me for another woman and they had a child, I would probably be hesitant in loving on that kid. I know it sounds un-Christian, but it's the truth.

But God is always present, working everything out for good.

As that eleven-year-old girl looked down on her

lifeless father lying on that ugly, blue carpet, she was hugged by another father who gave her Jesus' love.

Was my pain worth it? Was Charles's worth it? Is yours worth it? Based on the purpose described in 2 Corinthians, yes. Absolutely, yes.

CHAPTER 18

Make a Joyful Noise

If my life played out on the big screen, it would have the most amazing soundtrack. My earliest memories are associated with music. When I was a blonde, curly-headed three-year-old, Mama banged out Derek and the Dominos' "Layla" on her old upright while I sat beneath it and played with a green and purple My Little Pony named Peppermint Crunch.

"Susannah, get out from under there! It's too loud! I don't want your eardrums to bust!"

"I like it!" I squealed over the noise and brushed the plastic pony's tail as the vibrations of the piano strings rang through my soul.

My mother played by ear. Despite taking piano lessons for many years as a child, she couldn't read a note. When she made music, though, it was soulful and magical. It was amazing how she could hear a song one time and then sit on a piano bench and play it effortlessly. She played old gospel songs and Carole King and everything in between.

"Mama, play Mozart."

"Okay."

"Mama, play Metallica."

"Okay."

My mama and daddy loved making music together. Mama's voice harmonized well with his unmistakable sound as they strummed matching Yamaha guitars or played blues harps. One of my most prized possessions is the cassette tape I have of one of their many jam sessions in our living room. They chatter and laugh with friends between songs. My mother tells my daddy's best friend, David, that she heard he took Sybil out on a date last weekend. He says, "I don't want to talk about it, Susan Ann! Billy Brown, do 'Stairway to Heaven'!" I interrupt them a few times and ask for help reaching the VHS tape collection on the top bookshelf.

One Saturday night, before I even met Jason, I sat on Mama's bed with my daddy's old Yamaha and strummed the only five chords I know, but we managed to get about twelve Bob Dylan songs out of those chords. She sang while I played, just like she did with my father, and my old cassette player sat at the foot of the bed and recorded us.

We shared the piano bench after Christmas dinner and played a duet of "O Holy Night" while my brother, Keith, recorded us on his phone. In those moments, we not only made music together but we made so much joy and laughter. I knew one day she would be gone and I would cherish those recordings of us—just as I cherish the recordings of her and my father.

When I arrived at my mother's vacant house one January morning in 2016, the electricity had been turned off and the house was freezing. I pulled my coat close to my body and walked around the empty home. I peered into the kitchen and remembered the sound of bacon sizzling in a cast-iron skillet. I walked over to the dining room and remembered the last holiday meal we had at her table where I laughed so hard I choked on sweet tea. I peeked into the empty bedroom where my mama took her last breath. Nothing was in there now but a lone Kleenex wadded up in the spot where her bed used to be. And then I made my way to the living room. It was also empty except for the most important thing my mother owned—her baby grand piano.

When Mama bought the house years before, we sat on the plush, beige carpet in that bare living room, both of our bodies tanned from the summer sun, and we discussed where the piano should go.

"I think it would look best in front of the window." Mama's long, bouncy, blonde ponytail hung over her shoulder.

"This room has good acoustics." I echoed a few words.

And it did. Once the piano was moved in the house and placed in front of the large window, the sound of her fingers effortlessly playing Chopin or "What a Friend We Have in Jesus" reverberated off of the tall ceilings. Occasionally, I sat on the couch across from her, pulled out my phone, and recorded her on the piano bench. I was so proud of her talent, and most importantly, I still wanted to hear her play when the day came that she moved to the angels' choir.

On that cold January day, Mama had been in the angel's choir for nearly four months. I silently stared at the only thing left in the home, the baby grand, and a knot formed in my stomach. My thoughts were interrupted by the sound of the piano mover's large truck backing into the driveway. They would soon load up my mother's most prized possession, now my most prized possession, and move it to my sister's home because I didn't have room for the baby grand in my house.

Two men walked in with dollies and moving equipment and large blankets and immediately began disassembling the piano. This was nothing new to them. They moved pianos every day. But watching them remove the legs from that piano was a really big deal to me. It made me realize my mother would never play those eighty-eight keys again.

Within thirty minutes they were done, and the piano was loaded onto the truck with treble and bass clefs painted on the side. It disappeared down the road. Alone in the completely empty home, I fell to the living room floor where the piano had left indentions in the carpet. As I had so many times in the previous months, I cried. I buried my face into the soft carpet and cried nearly as much as I did when her body was lowered into the ground.

"Susannah, see if you recognize this one!" I could almost hear her say. And I envisioned her gracefully moving her freshly painted fingernails up and down the keyboard.

"'Shine on You Crazy Diamond' by Pink Floyd?"

I don't know how long I cried into the living room carpet. I don't know how long I spoke muffled words into the floor—apologies for my wrongs, things I never got the chance to say, requests for songs I never got the chance to record. When I was done, my face damp and swollen, I walked to the front door and called out, "Bye, Mama. Love you," as I had every time I left my mother's house.

Sometimes I sit on my back porch and watch the videos of my mother playing. I zoom in on her hands—the hands that held my own in parking lots when I was a child, the hands that packed my lunch for school, the hands that rested on the top of my head while blessings were prayed over my life. I often close my eyes and imagine I'm on her couch while she plays. I can almost smell the biscuits in the oven or the fabric softener in her washing machine. In some of the clips, I can hear my mother's pink fingernails clacking against the keys. Sometimes she pauses in the middle of the song to say, "Oh, darn. I messed up. You need to cut your fingernails, Susan." Only she knows she messed up; it sounded immaculate to me.

Where words fail, music often speaks. Hearing my parents sing and play invokes warm and peaceful feelings within that cannot adequately be described with words. Music even sparks creativity while I write. Right now, Ray Lamontagne plays on the speakers of my computer and leaves me searching for the right adjectives. I also listen to music when I work out because, let's face it, if nineties hip hop doesn't make you want to pick up the pace on an elliptical machine, nothing will.

So many songs are directly linked to my memories. My soundtrack, if you will. I'll never forget being seventeen years old and getting punched in the eye at a party while Pearl Jam's "Black" played. The Dixie Chicks take me back to my best friend's Nissan Sentra when we rode around after school. Bluegrass puts me back in my grandmother's kitchen. And Bob Dylan, every time, takes me back to our old living room with the corduroy couch and Quasar television and Atari in the corner.

Thankfully, my love of music and my mother's talent were passed on to my daughter. When she sits at Mama's baby grand, which has finally been moved to my living room, and she beautifully plays a classical piece that resounds throughout the room, I close my eyes. I picture my mama right there with us. I remember her sharing the bench with a two-year-old Natalie Ann and teaching her "Twinkle, Twinkle." Without a doubt, Mama would be so proud of the pianist her granddaughter has become.

The Bible instructs us to make a joyful noise. I didn't know that until I watched *Footloose* and Kevin Bacon told John Lithgow a thing or two. The Lord delights in music. Maybe not explicit lyrics about carjacking someone at a stoplight, but He delights when we sing praises to Him, even if we can't carry a tune in a bucket. He delights when we play instruments. He delights in my daughter sitting on my mother's piano bench. And I delight in it too.

At Mama's visitation, we were able to pull the audio from those many videos we'd recorded of her. When the funeral home finally cleared out that night, I sat alone in the parlor and looked at my beautiful mother in the casket. Over the speaker came a Willie Nelson melody that she'd played on my piano a few years earlier. I stood and walked over to her lying there, beautiful as ever, and I reached down and held her cold hand.

"These hands did some marvelous things," I whispered.

My mother is gone now, but her melody is still in my heart.

And it's a joyful noise.

CHAPTER 19

Keep On Keepin' On

My sweet granny, Rebecca, was one of my favorite people. Physically, she reminded me of Dorothy Zbornak from *The Golden Girls* with her gray English-lawyer mane and broad shoulder pads beneath silk blouses. She wore so many bracelets you could hear her jangling from a mile away. Her rouge and her lipstick always matched perfectly, which I found fascinating. She must've used the lipstick as rouge. It's the only logical explanation.

Every time Mama had to make a trip to the big bank downtown (with the waterfall in the lobby), we visited Granny's teller window. She stuffed a handful of suckers into the pockets of my bubble suit and showed me off to all of her friends at the bank. Before I left, she placed a lipstick kiss on my cheek, and we were suddenly wearing the same rouge.

When Granny retired from the bank, she volunteered all her time at the Golden Age Center. She spent countless hours at the center organizing events and fun outings for the spunky retirees in our county. She baked cakes, sold raffle tickets, served meals, and played Rook. She cut hearts out of construction paper to decorate the small cement building on Valentine's Day. She pulled the tree from the storage closet and adorned it with red and gold bows for Christmas.

After a day of volunteering, she cooked salmon patties and french fries in her spacious kitchen and danced to the bluegrass gospel playing on her antique transistor radio. Before bed, she pulled a can of Diet Coke and a yogurt from her "ice box" as a before-bed snack. Then she'd put on her gown and a hair net, slather her chest in Vicks, and watch Lorenzo Lamas in *Renegade* on the television with the bunny ears.

Every time the doors of Marvin's Chapel United Methodist Church were open, Granny was there. She sang a loud, joyful noise to the Lord in the choir, oftentimes off-key, and stayed after the service to pick up programs or hard-candy wrappers left in the pews. My grandmother was the busiest, most outgoing woman I knew.

And when my daddy, her only child, suddenly died, Granny didn't let up. No sir. She kept on rolling.

I spent a lot of time with Granny the summer after Daddy passed away. I spent the hot, humid days with her down at the center, entertaining the old folks with elementary songs I knew on the piano. I snuck Nilla Wafers from the kitchen and taped crepe paper to the cement block walls when we decorated for an octogenarian's birthday.

After a long summer day of blessing old folks with pudding cups and intense games of Scrabble, we spent the evening hours sitting on Granny's front porch. We cooled ourselves with cardboard fans and sipped Diet Cokes. Her friends stopped their cars in front of her house, rolled down the windows, and yelled at us from the street. Granny chattered and laughed with them until another car pulled up and honked for them to get the heck out of the way.

Some nights we went to Ms. Dora's or Mrs. Maxine's to play Rook. I soaked up the humor and wit and wisdom in those conversations as the Southern grandmothers gossiped and poured cans of Coke over ice. I scarfed down pounds of Chex Mix and nearly choked when Granny said something like, "Did you see Mary Martha's hat at church on Sunday? Lord have mercy, it looked like a traffic cone."

I had many wonderful memories at my granny's charming white house on the hill. I helped her shell peas and pick corn. I swayed on the porch swing while she push-mowed her yard in bare feet stained emerald green. I played in the shed behind her house where my dad had held practice for his band, the Shags, when he was in high school. I threw leftovers into the backyard for the birds and the neighbor's dog to gobble up.

Not long after my father died, Granny started hanging out with a new "friend" she met at the center. His name was Mr. Hardister and he drove a little Chevrolet Cavalier identical to my grandmother's car. I still smile when I think about those matching vehicles sitting side by side in her steep, gravel driveway. It was the cutest. Thing. Ever.

Mr. Hardister had been a widower for many years and owned a Lhasa Apso named Fuji. The dog survived on hot dogs and belly rubs. He resembled my Lhasa Apso quite a bit, but he had many more dental issues than my beloved Peaches. Fuji had what I liked to call "summer teeth." Some were here. Some were there. Fuji could also be kind of salty, but I didn't mind. He growled at me a few times, but at least he wasn't trying to rip my arm off like my aunt Cora's "Sweet Lady."

Fuji and I shared the back seat of Mr. Hardister's Cavalier as he drove us through the countryside. He told stories of his youth and talked about the ugliest woman he'd ever known. Her name was LuCindy and she had large, floppy ears like a bassett hound. Then he'd point out the driver's-side window and tell my grandmother, "Now, that's where Dale Bridges grew up. Right there in that wooden house." And Granny would point out the passenger-side window and say, "No, Prentice. He grew up in *that* wooden house." I didn't know Dale Bridges from Adam, and I didn't care where he grew up, but I sure enjoyed their banter.

On Saturday nights, we'd go with Mr. Hardister to little Podunk towns with names like Salisbury and Grand Junction to attend bluegrass gospel singings. Instead of dreading watching old men play fiddles and stomp their feet for two hours during my weekend, I relished in it. I'd get all filled with the Holy Spirit when they cranked out "I'll Fly Away" and lift my little thirteen-year-old hands in the air.

I delighted in every moment spent with my grand-mother. We both shared immense pain in losing a special man, my daddy, but we found so much joy together. I knew she was in deep mourning over the loss of her son. I saw the tears fall. I saw the grief in her eyes. But I also saw her plow straight through the heartache and loss, knowing she'd be reunited with Daddy someday. I saw her laugh with her friends at that kitchen table cov-ered in Rook cards. I saw her serve the little old ladies at the center who were grieving their own losses. I saw her minister to them with her servant's heart and her compassion and her own humor and wit. I saw her mow the grass in bare feet and talk about poor Mary Martha's hats. I watched her sing that bluegrass gospel, loud and off-key. I watched her keep on loving and keep on living.

My grandmother taught me grief is a place to visit, but it's not a place to stay.

She fought the battle of brokenness, armed with her Bible and her spunk. She'd say, "Don't feel sorry for me. I'm not pitiable. Everyone has gone through something, Susannah. Everyone fights some sort of battle. The way you know you've won the battle is if you come out stronger because of it."

As she aged, my heart broke watching my strong, independent grandmother wither away in a nursing home, her body riddled with colon cancer. We emptied her house on Watkins Street of her belongings, sold the dining room table where I'd eaten Christmas ham and mashed potatoes, helped load her antique lamps and "ice box" into the back of a stranger's truck. When it was apparent she could no longer live on her own and would have to stay in the home, we sold her charming white house on the hill. When I walked out her wrought-iron storm door for the last time when I was eighteen years old, I closed a door on my childhood.

On the day my grandmother died, when I was a few months pregnant with Natalie Ann, I mourned. But I also rejoiced. I rejoiced because I knew she was finally reunited with my father. I rejoiced because she had, indeed, persevered. I think of the words found in 1 Peter 5:10: "After you have suffered a little while, the God of all grace, who has called you to his eternal glory in Christ, will himself restore, confirm, strengthen, and establish you" (ESV).

I rejoiced because my grandmother was restored.

Strengthened. Established. After struggling with depression and loss on this earth, and then suffering through terribly aggressive cancer, she finally gained her everlasting prize—the everlasting crown. A crown that neither moth nor rust can destroy. The crown of eternal life.

Take a lesson from my sweet granny. Seek joy, wherever you can. Live. Laugh. Love. Persevere. Keep on keepin' on.

CHAPTER 20

Thank You for Bein' a Friend

One of my favorite parts of life is a bout of uncontrollable, eye-watering, bladder-clenching laughter. My gosh, I adore it. That's how I know when I've got a real good friend—when she can make me laugh so hard I have to clutch my stomach, bend over, and slap my knee while joy pours from my eyes.

The first friend I ever had who made me laugh that way was Kristen. We met in first grade and immediately hit it off. We laughed at random things no one else thought were funny. Kristen and I had the talent of getting tickled while in the worst places, like class or church or moments of silence. She would get to laughing, and then I would get to laughing, and one of us would have to excuse ourselves before we both ended up in detention.

Mama always knew when I was on the phone with Kristen. On the weekends in middle school, we'd call each other at 10:30 p.m. when *Mama's Family* was over. Mama would poke her head into my room and say, "Susannah, you've got to quiet down so I can get some sleep!" And then she'd poke her head into my room again ten minutes later and say, "It's time to tell Kristen good night."

Kristen and I were inseparable throughout our school years. We got in trouble for passing notes in class and cutting up about Coach Thomas's quiet, unintelligible voice. And once we were old enough to drive, we'd laugh so much that the driver would have to pull off for a pit stop at the Exxon bathroom because we just couldn't hold it any longer.

I looked forward to time spent with Kristen because I knew laughter was imminent. I knew a spit take was possible. I knew peeing in pants was inevitable. I craved it. I craved the inside jokes. I craved doubling over with tears pouring from my eyes. I craved being weak from laughter. I craved whatever nonsense we could get into on the weekends. I craved the joy we brought each other.

Kristen and I rarely hang out anymore because we are

both busy being wives and mothers, but when a text or instant message from her comes through, I know someone is going to eventually reply the laugh-cry emoji. We still share a beautiful bond of laughter.

My life has been abundantly blessed with some truly wonderful friends. I'm fortunate to associate with a group of women who always have an encouraging word. I'm fortunate to have friends to pray with and pray for. I'm thankful for the precious ladies I get to do life with. I'm thankful for their children being encouragers in my own children's lives.

When Mama died, so many stepped forward to lend a shoulder for me to cry on. The love of Christ was shown to me in multiple ways during that sorrowful period in my life. My mother was my spiritual mentor, but when she moved to heaven, the Lord was quick to place friends in my life who desired to mentor me spiritually—to encourage me and lift my spirits. Because God knows we need to be encouraged by each other's faith, just as Paul said in Romans 1:11–12 AMPC: "I am yearning to see you, that I may impart and share with you some spiritual gift to strengthen and establish you. That is, that we may be mutually encouraged and comforted by each other's faith, both yours and mine."

Paul had never even been to Rome when he wrote those powerful and promising words to the few hundred Christians who lived there. He'd met a handful of them on his travels, but he longed to introduce himself and share the good news of Christ not only to that handful of Christians, but to everyone in Rome—including those who had only heard gossip (some not so good) about him. Many Romans were non-Jews who were wondering what in the world the Jewish Messiah (who had lived, died, and been resurrected about thirty years before) had to do with them. Paul made it his mission to proclaim Christ's love to everyone, both Jew and Gentile.

Paul didn't even know these people, and yet he *yearned* to see them. He yearned to get to Rome and strengthen them and lift them up and love them. He wanted to watch them grow in their faith before his very eyes. And he needed them as much as they needed him.

Isn't that a beautiful depiction of friendship?

Yearning.

Yearning to spend time together. Yearning for conversation and fellowship. Yearning to share and impart. Yearning to love and lift. Yearning to share a spell of laughter. Yearning to offer inspiration and receive some too.

We are social creatures. We are most comfortable when we are surrounded by family and friends. Isn't this why we spend hours on Facebook? We long for a human connection (and to watch videos of cute dogs and find recipes). We long for like-minded individuals to show us kindness, empathy, and honesty.

We need people, y'all.

Friendship plays a vital role in a fulfilled and contented life. Those of us who are blessed with true friends, whether one or twenty, tend to be happier. There is nothing more satisfying than that bout of eye-watering laughter I mentioned earlier. Healthy friendship brings us joy, and that's exactly how God intends for it to be.

Ecclesiastes 4:9–10 tells us, "Two are better than one, because they have a good reward for their toil. For if they fall, one will lift up his fellow. But woe to him who is alone when he falls and has not another to lift him up!" (ESV).

Life ain't easy. We all fall and struggle at some point. So how wonderful it is to have a hand to help us up, a shoulder to cry on, a prayer partner to intercede to God on our behalf. And you know what? God places people in our life for these very reasons, just as he placed Kristen in my youth and some wonderful women in my adulthood as I grieved my mother. He knew I needed them. He knows we need each other. Proverbs 27:17 says, "As iron sharpens iron, so one person sharpens another."

True friendship is to encourage. To sympathize. To pass on the beautiful comfort that we receive not only from the Holy Spirit but from others. To truly love one another as God has loved us. To support. To yearn. To sacrifice.

Sacrifice.

This word appears 310 times in the King James version of the Bible. (I didn't count. I Googled.) Mr. Webster tells us that it means "destruction or surrender of something for the sake of something else: giving up of some desirable thing in behalf of a higher object."

So, what does sacrifice have to do with true friendship? *Everything.*

Jesus made the ultimate sacrifice for us. He laid down His life so that we can trust Him as our personal Savior and receive new life in Him. I like to consider myself a good friend. I send birthday texts and return books I've borrowed, but I've never hung bloody and beaten on a cross so that my friends would avoid eternal damnation!

To be a true friend, we must sacrifice. I'm sorry, but there's no getting around it. This means that our friendships are going to cost us something. Maybe friendship will cost us money or valuable time. Maybe it will cost us our pride. Maybe it will cost us our comfort. Maybe it will cost us dry-cleaning when we pee our pants. But guess what, ladies? Sacrifice ain't about us. It's about being obedient to the Lord, and the Lord calls us to sacrifice.

I forfeited sleeping in one Saturday morning because a dear sister needed to call and vent about her baby scribbling a Sharpie on the walls. That may not sound like a major sacrifice, but you just don't understand my love affair with sleep. Giving up an hour of slumber to listen to my friend cry and scrub her foyer with a Magic Eraser was a pretty big deal for me, okay?

But, in friendship, we are called to surrender what we

find valuable for something we consider to have a higher or more pressing claim—our friends. We are called to make ourselves accessible when it isn't convenient.

(And might I add that we are to joyfully sacrifice. Girls, we aren't to roll our eyes and huff and puff and complain because *Grey's* is about to come on but a friend has a flat tire on some dark back road and thinks she saw a werewolf.)

This. This is true friendship. Giving without wondering what you'll get in return. Taking a meal to the sick. Loving on the elderly. Forgetting ourselves in a self-serving world. Striving not only to assist our brothers and sisters, but most importantly to serve our Savior.

Maybe you're reading this and saying, "Well, I am a good friend. I joyfully sacrifice for friendship. I already know all this, Susannah."

Well, congratulations. But in John 15, Jesus said He is our friend too. Do we sacrifice our time to read His Word? Do we sacrifice some sweet sleep to attend church on Sunday morning? Do we sacrifice our pride when we're too embarrassed to share our faith with a nonbeliever? Do we sacrifice for the Lord?

Oh mercy. I'm so guilty of taking from our Savior and giving nothing in return.

When I was at a really cool record shop in Omaha last year, I approached the counter carrying a vintage U2 T-shirt and a Pearl Jam CD (because I only have eighteen Pearl Jam CDs). The clerk was a cool-looking guy with red spikey hair, tattoos, and a nose ring. When he asked what I did for a living, I told him I was a writer and podcaster.

"Oh, yeah? That's cool. What's your podcast about?"

"It's a women's podcast," I said.

I deliberately left out one word. It's a *Christian* women's podcast. Why did I do that? Because I thought a guy with a pierced septum would think I was weird for being a Christian.

As soon as I walked out of that store, I felt lower than the rent on a burning building. If I'd told him what my podcast was really about, it could have opened up a whole discussion about the Lord. Or the guy may have been a believer and shared his faith with me. Just because he worked in a record store and had hair the color of the Kool-Aid man doesn't mean he wasn't a Christian.

I didn't sacrifice my pride for Jesus, and He deserves the most sacrifice of all.

Satan doesn't like when we acknowledge our good Friend, Jesus. And not only that, but he doesn't like it one bit when sisters in Christ come together to pray over their marriages and their children. He doesn't like it when we do life together. He is threatened by friendship and will gladly throw a little drama in the mix. He will let a petty argument over a borrowed Tupperware dish or a catty remark about an outfit fester. He loves to pull a Yoko Ono and break up the group.

Kristen and I may not ride around every weekend

listening to the Dixie Chicks and laughing our butts off anymore, but we never let the Enemy break us up even though he attempted to many times. We fought for our friendship and held on to it without the option of letting go.

Because that's just how important friendship is.

CHAPTER 21

Whoa! Slow Down

Each morning, within five seconds of waking, my mind goes into overdrive. I immediately begin stewing about the tasks before me. Since I usually oversleep, this only adds to the urgency in my head. It's like I have a hamster on a spinning and smoking wheel up there, racing and panting his little heart out.

I'm a goal-oriented person, and I live my life by lists. I don't know how to live without them. Nothing gives me more satisfaction than scratching off one of the day's many chores. When I *really* want to feel accomplished, I'll add something I've already done to the list just to feel the gratification of marking it off.

But as soon as I've scratched a thick, dark line through one chore or goal on the wide-ruled notebook paper, I add three other things to it. Some days I swear I will never catch up.

Each time the phone rings or chimes, I'm alerted to jot down another thing. Deadlines, speaking events, church functions, the kids' extracurricular activities, and sports practices all rest on my calendar. I should probably pencil in a time to go grocery shopping too, because we can't split that lone, frostbitten fish stick on the freezer floor four ways.

I really should organize the hall closet, clean the fridge, and finish reading that book I downloaded on my Kindle four years ago. The car may abruptly ignite into a heaping fireball if I don't find the time to get the sludgy six-month-old oil changed. And I need to kill the dust armadillos under the couch and find the pair of shoes Natalie Ann misplaced in the fall of 2014. I mean, I know she can't wear them anymore, but I'd like to know what in the world happened to them and maybe get ten bucks for them on eBay.

Our society praises those who are always on the go, always texting, talking, and scheduling on the phone. It's difficult to fully enjoy a movie or quiet time or a good book because our minds are elsewhere.

When several of my videos went viral, I was more overwhelmed than ever. It seemed everyone wanted something from me. On top of all my usual responsibilities such as getting the kids to practice, cooking supper, doing laundry, scheduling orthodontist appointments, writing columns, and keeping the dogs alive, I was suddenly a "public figure" who had to be "on" all the time. I had to have new jokes. I had to be inspirational. I had to give a speech. Sign some books. Appear at a charity event. Call in to a radio show. And yes, appear on the Weather Channel to talk about my video on ball moms being the best meteorologists. (I don't think we'll be able to play ball tomorrow. Variable clouds early with thunderstorms in the afternoon. Winds southwest at fifteen miles per hour.)

One afternoon I sat on my couch and thought on all the blessings and opportunities the Lord had given me. I never thought a video of me sitting in the car (not wearing makeup or a bra) while I whined about my youngest child going to kindergarten would be seen by more than fifty million people. I never thought that video would grow my platform and open so many doors for my writing and speaking career. I was so incredibly thankful for each and every opportunity, and I wanted to be obedient to Him and walk the path He placed before me, but I was dadgum overwhelmed. I felt pulled in a million different directions, and I'm no Stretch Armstrong. I knew I was going to break because my plate was not just full—it was overflowing.

When I was about twelve years old, I stood in my granny's bathroom and admired all her makeup and jewelry sitting on her vanity. Granny, a devout Methodist, had dozens of Upper Room pamphlets in a basket on the floor next to the counter. I picked one up, and as I flipped through, I was mesmerized by a particular picture. In black and white, it was a sketch of Jesus on the throne. Dozens of men and women and children relaxed at His feet above the scripture from Matthew, "Come to me all who are weary and heavy-laden, and I will give you rest."

As a twelve-year-old writer, I was utterly fascinated by the words "heavy laden." I said them over and over as I stared at the photo.

It was no accident I found that scripture and photo only a year after my daddy had passed away and I was so incredibly weary and heavy laden. I tore the page from the pamphlet and took it home. It hung on my bedroom corkboard for years, and I still have it in a box in my attic.

While sitting on my couch that afternoon, overwhelmed with the million different directions I was being pulled, I recalled that scripture and sketch and envisioned myself resting at Jesus' feet. I cast all my burdens on Him—the anxiety and stress that accompanied my success and the still-fresh emotional burden of losing my mother. And I rested.

And what sweet relief it was.

I've learned that sometimes we have to say no to events or things presented to us. Must we go to every party and social event we've been invited to attend?

Must we show up for every extracurricular activity? Our society says we should. If we don't follow through with commitments, we are labeled as lazy slackers with no motivation or purpose.

What if we could skip a couple of unnecessary appointments for the sake of our sanity and not be judged for it or feel pangs of guilt? What if the solution is to just say no? What if the answer is to quit committing to every email, text message, or slip of paper that arrives in our children's school planners?

Yes.

Okay.

I'll be there.

I can do that.

No problem.

How often do we utter those words for fear of hurting another's feelings, when the only ones we're hurting are ourselves? How often do we commit to things out of guilt instead of dedication or genuine excitement? Oh, Lord. I used to be so guilty of it. I was riding high on the whirlwind. I was overbooking myself and missing my children's ball games and steak dinners with my husband. I was worn and weary and even lacked joy in writing—the one thing that's always brought me such happiness. Everything was out of balance.

But now I've embraced a sweet truth prompted by that powerful verse in Matthew. If I don't feel the Lord has placed a specific thing in my path, I turn it down. I leave some room on my plate. Room for dessert, if you will. Room for the sweet, relaxing moments. I prioritize now: my relationship with the Lord first, then my family, and then my career.

I rest.

(And you know what? God Himself rested on the seventh day. What makes us think we don't need to?)

It's not possible for most working women to take more than two weeks of rest at a time. As a writer, I am fortunate to be able to set my own hours. Maybe you cannot do that, but you can prioritize your lives. You can figure out what's really important. You can make some lists. You can say no.

You can rest.

CHAPTER 22

Not Crazy, Not Absurd, Simply Beautiful!

While a dear friend and I were hanging out on my patio one summer night, she said, "Susannah, tell me a story. Tell me one of your funny stories."

I wasn't sure where to start.

When the stranger in Walmart asked me to check the size tag on her underwear? Or maybe the one about the lady who was wearing Marvin the Martian pajama pants in Petco and asked me to hold her overactive Chihuahua while she searched her purse for her checkbook? "She may pee on you, but it'll only be a dribble."

Do you want to hear the story about my daddy riding on the outside of the train again? When Aunt Cora's feist gnawed on Uncle Harvell's artificial leg while we watched *The Newlywed Game*? The time aliens visited my dog? Or when I was nearly killed on a horse? Did I tell you the one about the dead chicken hatching on our Thanksgiving table?

Wait! Did I already tell you about the time someone tried to break into our house but slid on a frozen pile of dog poop in our driveway and was apprehended by the police? The copperhead snake coiled up behind our refrigerator? When my mama drove her Buick into a river? When my daddy drove his Chevrolet into a river? When I drove a golf cart into a river?

Do you know about the fistfight I got in at a high school party where I was thrown into the deep end of a pool? When I almost missed my high school graduation because I had detention? Or the time I touched the hem of Fred Durst's Dickies at a Limp Bizkit concert? When I contracted mange from a dumpster dog and had to stay in the hospital? When I lost my entire kneecap after a rollerblading accident? Oh, that's a good one.

When my mama prayed life over our brown labrador, Hershey, after he drank antifreeze? I'll be darned if that dog didn't fully recover after her petition to God! What about the time a woodchuck was stuck on the limb outside our front door and prohibited us from going on the porch for two days? The time our four-wheeler flew out of the bed of the truck while Jason was driving? The time the owl flew into the side of my car? I once fell into some bushes on the playground and was stuck there until lunchtime.

"Susannah, you're making that up!" My friend laughed.

"You can't make this stuff up," I answered.

My life is riddled with crazy, absurd stories that couldn't be made up. And good Lord, I'm thankful for it. Because when someone asks me to tell them a story, I've got plenty of material.

But you know what else you can't make up? It's not absurd. It's not crazy.

It's beautiful.

It's life-changing.

It's the best story I know.

"For God so loved the world that he gave his one and only Son, that whoever believes in him shall not perish but have eternal life. For God did not send his Son into the world to condemn the world, but to save the world through him" (John 3:16–17).

Those words have been ingrained in our minds since we were children. Sweet Sunday school teachers had us highlight John 3:16 in our Bibles. Vacation Bible school teachers had us put the words on crafts made of Popsicle sticks. For many of us, it is the first Bible verse, the first truth, we ever learned. We are reminded of John 3:16 on billboards and T-shirts and bumper stickers. And that's a wonderful thing.

But have we become desensitized to the powerful truth found in the book of John? Do we even realize the magnitude of God's love? Or has it become a nice little verse we learned as children?

As believers, we should never become bored or numb to this beautiful reality. We should always bask in joy that God, the creator of the heavens and the earth, sent His only Son to die on a cross for us.

For us.

For every sin we've ever committed.

For every sin we haven't committed yet.

God saw that the law wasn't working. People couldn't successfully follow the rules and regulations of the old covenant. They were offering burnt sacrifices left and right but were not capable of maintaining perfection through the old law. And when the time was right, because of His unfailing compassion for us, God changed all the rules and regulations. He made the ultimate sacrifice by sending Jesus to die for our sin. And not only that, but to free us from condemnation and guilt and addiction and affliction and every other stronghold we encounter in this fallen world.

John 3:19 reads, "This is the verdict: Light has come into the world, but people loved darkness instead of light because their deeds were evil." And that's the very reason the people chose Jesus over Barabbas, a murderer and thief, to die on the cross—a manner of death reserved for the lowliest criminals. And we continue to choose

Barabbas every single day, don't we? We choose the ways of the world. We choose our flesh. Our desires. Our sin. Continually, that's what we choose. And yet, praise God, our sins are atoned for.

We are pardoned because Jesus, bloodied and beaten, bore His cross to Golgotha. Nails were driven through His wrists and ankles. And then the cross was erected, and Jesus, blameless, was on that hill for the masses to see—for the masses to ridicule and spit on. He had the power to remove Himself from that cross, but He didn't. He hung there for you and me.

How can we not be passionate about the most powerful love story to ever occur? How do we become used to the ultimate sacrifice that took place on that old, rugged cross? How are we insensitive to the burden Jesus bore? We forget His last moments of torment when He asked His Father, "Why have You forsaken Me?" We forget the bloodshed. We forget the earth rumbling and the heavens breaking open. We forget the greatest example of *agape* love.

Don't you know this just tickles Satan? He does not want us to realize God's prevailing love for us. He wants us to believe Jesus' death wasn't all it's cracked up to be, or that it's not even true. And if it is true, we are too dirty, too unclean, too sinful to accept God's mercy and grace. We are too "bad" to benefit from what was done on the cross that day. Satan doesn't want us to see the extent of what happened at Golgotha. And we too often fall for it.

Sister, my prayer is that you fully realize the scale of God's love for you. I pray you envision and understand what God's precious and blameless Son went through for you. *Yes, you.* God's heart must have been grieved at Jesus' pain and suffering, yet He did what had to be done to save you.

It is love at its finest and purest and most powerful.

The truth found in the book of John isn't just a Bible verse to memorize or something you see on a billboard on a busy interstate. It is the truth that saves souls from hell and sets captives free. It is the good news. The best news. The ultimate news.

And it's about you.

Forget your flaws.

Forget your hang-ups.

Forget your sin.

God did. God forgot all of it the moment you recognized what Jesus did on that cross and you asked Him into your heart.

You are loved immensely and immeasurably. No matter what you've gone through in this life, joy is attainable through Jesus.

You can't make *that* up.

Acknowledgments

If a hip-hop artist who just won the "Most Explicit Album" award thanks God first, then of course I must too. I thank Him for seeing me through every struggle and restoring my joy time and time again. He is good and worthy to be praised.

Much thanks to Jessie Kirkland for seeing potential in me, helping me brainstorm, and giving me great advice and wisdom on this journey. The goal of every video I made and blog post I wrote was to catch the attention of an agent, and I'm surely glad I caught the attention of such a good one.

Thank you to my Thomas Nelson team—Jenny, Stephanie, Janene, Sara, and those I've never even met— who helped make my first work of nonfiction a reality. You're good people.

I'm so incredibly thankful for the support of my husband, Jason; my children; and my mother-in-law, Kristi, who are always proud of me and proud for me.

And, of course, a big shout out to every single person on the World Wide Web for the likes, shares, follows, comments, and support. I would still be tossing my writings into a Rubbermaid tote, never to be read by another soul, if I hadn't been encouraged by so many strangers to keep going. You're good people too.

My prayer is this book will draw everyone who reads it closer to Jesus. He *is* the upside to life's downs.

To Mama, Daddy, Mr. Charles, my grandparents, and my precious Nutella who sat right beside me while I wrote every word of this book—I love you with my heart and can't wait to get to heaven to see you all again.

About the Author

Susannah B. Lewis is an author, blogger, and humorist. She's had several articles and videos go viral and has been featured in Erma Bombeck's Humor Writers, *Parents* magazine, *US Weekly*, and *Reader's Digest*. Susannah lives with her husband, children, and dogs in Tennessee. You can find her online and on social media @whoasusannah.